# Voices fron

## An Anthology o.

### 1549–1928

Alan M. Kent was born in St Austell and grew up in the china clay mining region of mid-Cornwall. In addition to being a poet, novelist and dramatist, he has a number of academic publications to his name. In 1998 he was awarded a doctorate for his research into Cornish, Cornu-English and Anglo-Cornish literature. His study *Writing Cornwall: Continuity, Identity, Difference* will be published later this year. He is currently completing a new verse adaptation of the Cornish mystery play trilogy known as *Ordinalia*.

Bernard Deacon was born and brought up Cornwall. He is a Lecturer in Regional History for Exeter University in Cornwall, an Associate Lecturer in Social Sciences for the Open University and author of several publications on aspects of Cornish history and contemporary Cornish society. He is currently researching the subject of Cornish identity between 1750 and 1870.

Alan M. Kent

# Voices from West Barbary

## An Anthology of Anglo-Cornish Poetry 1549–1928

Edited with an introduction by Alan M. Kent

Foreword by Bernard Deacon

Francis
Boutle
Publishers

First published by Francis Boutle Publishers
23 Arlington Way
London EC1R 1UY
Tel/Fax: (020) 7278 4497
Email: fbp@francisboutle.demon.co.uk
www.francisboutle.demon.co.uk

ISBN 0 9532388 8 1

Printed in Great Britain by Redwood Books

*To my mother and my father
and days on Halveggan Downs*

# Contents

# Foreword

**Bernard Deacon**

In this book we hear the voices of a largely forgotten culture. For the Cornish, geographical marginality has been magnified by cultural marginality, one of the penalties of living next to a large and dominant culture. Moreover, an inclination to romanticise has added a large quota of the ridiculous and the plain confusing to images of Cornwall. Generations of Cornish children learnt that they inhabited a place once known as West Barbary, a romantically different, backward and uncivilised place, the haunt of strange people, smugglers, wreckers and other assorted quaint characters.

The classic definition of West Barbary views it as a product of the eighteenth and early nineteenth centuries. The English at that time represented, or misrepresented, the Cornish as barbarous inhabitants of a primitive land, comparing it to the Barbary coast of North Africa, from where pirates had periodically descended on local shipping in the Western Approaches before the mid-seventeenth century. The foreign 'other' was transmuted into an 'other' within. In this construction the Cornish seem to be the passive victims, the people on the periphery defined by a culturally more powerful centre. But was this the case? Alan M. Kent sets out in this anthology to reclaim the term West Barbary and use it to re-emphasise Cornish difference. And this is exactly what the Cornish also did two hundred years ago in what was, arguably, the most creative period in their history. Indeed, I would go further. The Cornish of the early nineteenth century did not just reclaim the myth of West Barbary; to a large extent they invented it.

When we pursue this metaphor of West Barbary it turns out to be tantalisingly elusive. In the oft-quoted account by mining historian A.K. Hamilton Jenkin of a London visitor in the 1770s it is Hamilton Jenkin himself and not the Londoner who uses the actual words. Later accounts regularly assert that Cornwall was described in this way by people east of the Tamar, yet actual examples of this description in contemporary writings of those 'east of the Tamar' are not so easy to find. But there are many cases of Cornish writers claiming West Barbary was a common description. One, Sarah Gregor, wrote in her memoirs in the 1860s that it was 'an epithet which still prevailed in my youth'. But in writings on Cornwall by both Cornish and English in the eighteenth century West Barbary is strangely absent. William Borlase, writing in the *Universal*

*Magazine* in 1758, makes no mention, instead stating that 'the Cornish people, as to their manners, are generally allowed to be civil and courteous to strangers'.

Borlase's words, perhaps unexpected in a local man, were an early example of how others were tending to describe the Cornish by the 1790s. What most often struck the outside observer was not the 'barbarity' of the Cornish but the ingenuity, enterprise and sobriety of its population, and in particular its mining population. For the Cornish in the eighteenth century had built, on the twin foundations of deep metal mining and the steam engine, one of Europe's first industrial regions. In the first half of the 1800s its people were being held up as models for others. In 1846 the social commentator J.D.Tuckett, in *A History of the Past and Present State of the Labouring Population,* was describing the Cornish miners as presenting 'by many degrees the brightest picture we have met, of the condition of any considerable body of the labouring class in England'.

The dominant myth of the Cornish, by the 1840s and 1850s held by both outsiders and insiders, therefore seems to class them as part of 'industrial civilisation'. However, from this grew the, at first sight, paradoxical need to recover the older image. And this need was felt most strongly by the Cornish themselves. For myths of 'industrial civilisation' and narratives of achievement required a point of comparison in order to measure the progress. The representation of Cornwall as West Barbary fitted perfectly. Indeed, in the retelling of the myth of 'industrial civilisation' West Barbary became more barbarian and 'industrial civilisation' more civilised. The Cornish reaffirmed the existence of a former West Barbary and constantly referred to it in their writings of the early nineteenth century and in a very real sense, therefore, the myth was a local creation, part of the search for difference and a point of contrast for the industrial, Methodist Cornish of the mid-nineteenth century.

With the collapse of industry in the later nineteenth century Cornwall was reinvented, in another version of romanticism, as a 'delectable Duchy'. While Cornish writers such as Arthur Quiller Couch also contributed to this construction they were never the dominant creators of it. New layers of meaning were superimposed upon Cornwall and the active role of Cornish people as active agents in reproducing the myth of West Barbary was lost. However, the Cornish continued to negotiate and transform romantic images for their own purposes. This book recovers their voices. Its title serves to remind us of the active role that the Cornish played in the construction of romantic myths. Unheard they might have been; passive victims they were not.

# Preface

This anthology gathers together for the first time in one collection the riches of Anglo-Cornish poetry from the Renaissance to the beginning of the twentieth century. Its time-span extends from the 1549 Prayer Book Rebellion to the first Cornish Gorseth of 1928 and it makes representative and important pieces of verse from the Anglo-Cornish literary continuum available for both the general and academic reader. As well as the better known figures of the tradition, Sidney Godolphin, Henry Quick, Robert Stephen Hawker and John Harris, the anthology introduces poets such as John Tabois Tregellas, James Dryden Hosken and W. Herbert Thomas, who though now hidden among the literary debris of the past, were important shapers of the poetic history of Cornwall.

In making my selection I have taken account of accessibility, length and the contribution of the poets to the construction of Cornish identity. Most space is given to those poets who seem to me, and to others, to be the best – Harris, Hawker and Hosken. Where possible I have tried to redress past inattention and have included a number of previously under-represented women poets as well as several anonymous broadsheet pieces that bring us the real sound of the working-class voice of Cornwall.

I would like to thank the publishers J.M. Dent for their permission to publish poems by James Dryden Hosken from the book *Shores of Lyonesse*, Audrey Pool for allowing me to use P.A.S. Pool's edited versions of the poems of Henry Quick and G.S. Symondson for granting.permission to publish poems by Arthur Quiller Couch. Every effort has been made to seek permissions from publishers and authors' estates and I would like to thank the Society of Authors for their assistance.

Considering the breadth of a volume of this kind, there are numerous scholars, colleagues and friends to thank. Among these are Charles Thomas, Amy Hale, Les Goldman, Tim Saunders, Andrew Symons, John Sansom, James Whetter, Neil Kennedy, Melissa Hardie, John Rowe, David Everett, Derek Williams, Angela Broome of the Courtney Library, Royal Institution of Cornwall, Truro, Kim Cooper and Joanne Hillman of the Cornish Studies Library, Redruth, Roger Toy and Don Hutchinson of King Arthur's Halls of Chivalry, Tintagel, Jane Colliver of the Newlyn Art Gallery, Annabelle Read and the staff of the Morrab Library, Penzance, Cambridge University Library and Colin Edwards of the County Records Office, Truro. Finally, my sincere thanks to Bernard Deacon for his perceptive foreword and also to Clive Boutle and David Russell at Francis Boutle Publishers.

# Introduction

West Barbary, a term frequently used to describe Cornwall during the eighteenth and nineteenth centuries, seems an appropriate title for a collection of this kind, because of the way it paradoxically delineates Cornish difference and identity over time. Outside observers two hundred years ago viewed Cornwall as a place of food riots and lawlessness, of wrecking and smuggling. A myth developed: Cornwall was a barbarous place in the west of the islands of Britain. One London visitor who came to Cornwall in 1775 thought the 'natives' of Cornwall were most contented when

they can sit down to a furze blaze, wringing their shirts and pouring the mud and water out of their boots. But the common people here are very strange kind of beings, half savages at the best. Many thousands of them live entirely underground, where they burrow and breed like rabbits. They are as rough as bears, selfish as swine, obstinate as mules, and hard as the native iron.[1]

A century later, in 1879, the myth of the 'strange' and 'primitive' Cornish man and woman was being perpetuated; this time by Robert Louis Stevenson in his book *Across the Plains*:

There were no emigrants direct from Europe – save one German family and a knot of Cornish miners who kept grimly to themselves, one reading the New Testament all day long through steel spectacles, the rest discussing privately the secrets of their old-world mysterious race. Lady Hester Stanhope believed she could make something of the Cornish; for my part, I can make nothing of them at all. A division of races, older and more original than Babel, keeps this close, esoteric family apart from neighbouring Englishmen. Not even a Red Indian seems more foreign in my eyes. This is one of the lessons of travel – that some of the strangest races dwell next door to you at home.[2]

So pervading was this myth that it was even used as a way of describing Cornwall in W. Herbert Thomas' influential 1892 collection of Anglo-Cornish poetry *Poems of Cornwall*.[3] In essence what Thomas and all the earlier observers were commenting on was Cornish difference, Celtic 'Otherness' on the margins. Even as late as 1908, the writer and naturalist W. H. Hudson commented on how a Cornish farmer reminded him of 'an orang-utan' with 'long monkey-like arms', 'pouring out a torrent of gibberish'.[4] Other Celtic peoples of these islands had, of course, been characterised in similar tones. Indeed Matthew Arnold (whose mother was Cornish) believed that the Celts, though a wild and imaginative group, needed, in their own interest, to be kept in check.[5] In many ways therefore, despite being a myth, the term 'West Barbary' fits much of the imaginative construction of Cornwall in past centuries and we feel justified in reclaiming it here.

However, in order to understand the voices of the poets in this anthology, there is a second myth we need to deal with, one perpetuated in Cornwall itself. It says that prior to the Tudor period, there was a kind of Cornish-language 'Eden', that was followed (at least until the Revival of the early twentieth century) by a steady decline into the oblivion of English speech and writing, eroding and destroying Cornish identity. This myth is an all too essentialist view of Cornish history for it neglects to celebrate the real picture that existed between 1549 and 1928. In fact, before this period, while Cornish remained the core language of the people, numerous other tongues were spoken. Among these were Latin, French, Breton and English.[6] Such a multilingual community reflects Cornwall's multiculturalism, and should be seen as a corrective to the vision of a peripheral, marginal society. On the western seaboard, Cornwall not only formed a link between other territories to the north and south, but was also on numerous occasions the starting point for maritime exploration.

The fate of Cornwall's linguistic and literary development had, however, been sealed just as this volume begins. Much has been written on the consequences of the 1497 Cornish rebellions against Tudor centralism,[7] but it was the Act of Uniformity of 1549 and its aftermath which did most to alter the cultural landscape of Cornwall. Though previous Kings and governments had given Cornwall special dispensation, this time it too had to conform to the edicts of the 'centre'. When the *Book of Common Prayer* made it clear that Cornish was not to be used in church services the leaders of the Prayer Book Rebellion declared that 'we the Cornish men (whereof certain of us understand no English) utterly refuse this new English'.[8] Their appeal was rebuffed and when the rebellion failed, thousands of Cornish men were killed by Sir Anthony Kingston, the Provost Marshall.[9] This atmosphere is reflected in our first writer here, Andrew Boorde, who in a poem published just two years earlier captures an image of the conventional Cornishman off to London in an act of rebellion. Though it is essentially comic, the piece had more serious undertones.

After the failure of the Prayer Book Rebellion the English language began a period of ascendancy in Cornwall. The writers Nicholas Roscarrock and Richard Carew exemplify the tensions in Cornish literary culture from that period to the present. Roscarrock was a folklorist and a hagiographer, interested in sustaining and keeping alive the older saintly traditions of Cornwall. A Catholic who refused to submit to the Reformation, he probably had knowledge of the continuum of Cornish drama and was certainly aware of Cornish language and literature. To this extent, Roscarrock prefigures a number of literary movements in Cornwall. They include the school of writers made up principally of John Keigwin, the Boson family, Thomas Tonkin and William Gwavas active in the late seventeenth and early eighteenth centuries,[10] as well as those scholars such as W. S. Lach-Szyrma, Henry Jenner and Robert Morton

Nance who were so crucial to the late nineteenth and early twentieth century Revival of Cornish.[11] Carew, however, took a different line. Although born just after the Act of Uniformity, he foresaw the shift in language and culture in Cornwall. In his influential essay 'The Excellency of the English Tongue' he welcomed the sophistication which English would offer, not only to the people of Cornwall, but to other cultures as well.[12] And indeed it was not long before the 'English Tongue' was used to reassert a renewed and confident Cornish identity. Even the English poet Michael Drayton was to depict a confident and powerful Cornwall in his epic *Poly-Olbion*.

Much study has been made of the number of people speaking Cornish at particular times in history, though there has been suprisingly little sociolinguistic investigation of the moments of language transfer. How did Cornish speakers actually lose their language? How did they gain English? Were the two spoken side-by-side, sentence-by-sentence? Why did particular Cornish words, expressions and idioms survive into Cornu-English, and others fall by the wayside? To be sure, these questions are problematical. However, just to start thinking about them allows us to perceive the real process of language shift, and understand much of what underlies the verse collected in this volume.

The collection runs from the Renaissance, when the multicultural Cornwall first begins to be transformed, to the founding of the first Cornish Gorseth in 1928. The latter seems a fitting point to stop, for 1928 saw the barding of the Anglo-Cornish writers Sir Arthur Quiller Couch and James Dryden Hosken. The Gorseth also marked a change in the cultural situation for Cornwall. The decline of the Cornish language since 1549 was being reversed. The immediate period after the first Gorseth too saw the rise of new Anglo-Cornish writers such as A.L. Rowse, Charles Causley and Jack Clemo and the beginning of another phase of literature.

After the Reformation, the next decisive phase of Cornish history was the period of the Civil War, exemplified in the work of Sidney Godolphin. A striking gap is then seen – that phase of Cornish history from around 1650–1750 which seems the most difficult to grasp, partly because of the lack of surviving texts. Recovery from the aftermath of the Civil War, and mediation between the Cornish and English traditions form part of the background, as does the process of proto-industrialisation. To a certain extent, Cornwall had always been industrial. Herodotus details the trades made with the 'islands of tin', and yet in the period in which writers such as Thomas Hogg, Humphry Davy, George Woodley and Henry Quick were writing, Cornwall underwent massive economic and social change. Quick's naïve verse in particular reflected this process, while in the face of modernisation Hogg, Davy and Woodley looked to a grander romantic past. The tension which had begun with Roscarrock and Carew thus continued on into the nineteenth century. John Tabois Tregellas echoed the voice of the emergent industrial era, whilst Francis Hingeston, Charles Taylor Stephens and John Abraham appeared to look for solace in the Cornish landscape – by now starting to attract visitors from elsewhere in search of picturesque scenery. The metal mines too attracted visitors, but others were more critical. Robert Stephen Hawker's verse regretted what he considered to be the twin evils of industrialisation and that other core construct for Cornish people of this period – Methodism. Elsewhere the finest depiction of these twin constructs is found in the verse of John Harris, William Bentinck Forfar and Charles Chorley. Poets such as the folklorist Robert Hunt and Henry Sewell Stokes still preferred to imagine past Cornwalls, even though they were both involved professionally in the modernisation process.

Even in the remarkable verse of John Harris, the first signs of the decay and decline of industrialisation are touched upon. Anglo-Cornish poetry then moved into a new phase, which reflected the concerns of both the Cornish at home having to subsist in what was rapidly becoming one of the first post-industrial societies, and of those many thousands of Cornish who went overseas – to North and South America, Australia and South Africa – in search of a better life and employment. While poets such as Mark Guy Pearse and Katharine Lee Jenner depicted this process, others including Joseph Thomas, reminded people how wonderful life back home could be. Certainly during this phase some of the verse was sentimental, yet that was its purpose; to remind the miner stuck in some hot shaft in Australia of life back home in Redruth or St Just-in-Penwith. The culmination of this genre is contained in W. Herbert Thomas' volume,[13] which seemed almost to serve as a literary reminder of how sweet home could be, and gave those emigrants scattered across the globe hope that one day they might return and that the collapse of industrialisation might somehow be just a temporary blip in Cornish history. An awareness of Cornish achievement overseas and in world history is also seen in the work of poets like Ernest L.T. Harris-Bickford, who considered the fate of the explorer of Africa, Richard Lander.

There was a corresponding and growing awareness that in order to survive the twentieth century Cornwall would somehow need to re-invent itself. This re-invention took two courses. First of all, as a consequence of the work of figures such as Margaret Ann Courtney and Robert Hunt (not to mention the other important collectors H.J. Whitfeld and William Bottrell [14]), the act of folklore collecting was no longer seen as an antiquarian process alone. The collecting of Cornish material would in the future be used as a means of revival and development – not just for curious interest. That way, Cornwall could ensure its voice in what appeared to many observers, as an unstoppable Anglicisation. In Cornwall, as in other Celtic territories, this was attributed to the gaining of ground by new media, widely circulated newspapers and radio. The poetry of Katharine Lee Jenner and James Dryden Hosken therefore did much to reassert Cornish difference, aligning itself with the past. Their poetry certainly reflects the wider concerns of the Cornish Revival in this period, yet for their 'revivalist' contemporaries such as W. S. Lach-Szyrma, Henry Jenner and Robert Morton Nance, the Anglo-Cornish continuum appeared not to represent 'true' and 'authentic' Cornwall. The vision of a revived Cornish language and literature was commendable, yet it failed (in this phase at least) to grasp the nettle of communicating the importance of that vision to the vast majority of Cornish people, who still regarded the Cornish dialect of English as their central symbol of identity. To be fair to Nance, he had initially tried in his *Cledry Plays* to promote this genre,[15] yet the process of the revival of the Cornish language would take much longer.

The other approach to re-invention was through tourism, which had its literary beginnings in the seventeenth and eighteenth centuries with the observations on Cornwall of travellers such as Celia Fiennes and Daniel Defoe.[16] It was then stimulated by others interested in the landscape and scenery and in the opening decades of the twentieth century developed by the railway companies.[17] The railway companies marketed Cornwall as a legendary land, where folklore could still be found around every corner. The barbarous land of yesteryear had been sanitised, however, and made attractive for those who wished to escape metropolitan England. Even the menacing wreckers and smugglers had been assigned to romance largely due to the fictions of nineteenth-century novelists working in Cornwall and outside.

One issue that faces anyone interested in Cornish literary culture is that of terminology. This anthology contains a selection of Anglo-Cornish verse. By that I mean Cornish verse written in English, yet this too has its own internal labelling problem. Within the wider field of Cornish verse written in English some might be designated 'dialect verse', an unsatisfactory term since it demeans the singularity and power of that mode of expression for Cornish people in the past and today. Perhaps a better label is Cornu-English, conveying the specific and significant nature of the genre within the wider field of Anglo-Cornish verse. As we shall see, the label is even more important when one considers the considerable number of Cornish language words and expressions which came to be incorporated into the genre.[18] Cornu-English vernacular has been badly neglected in the overall history of Cornwall, even though it remains the main mode of expression for many Cornish people.[19] The examples in this book from John Tabois Tregellas, William Sandys, William Bentinck Forfar and Joseph Thomas could be the basis for a re-evaluation. Except by some contemporary Cornish writers [20] Cornu-English has all too often been consigned to the culturally-restricted world of dialecticians and comedians. It demands more respect and understanding.

Another issue is that of the woman's voice in Cornish and Anglo-Cornish poetry. Apart from a few preliminary investigations,[21] few issues of feminism or gender have been explored by Cornish scholars. Again, this book offers a corrective by including work by important nineteenth and twentieth-century poets such as Margaret Ann Courtney, Katharine Lee Jenner and Annie E. Argall. Since at first sight much of the trappings of Cornish history and culture, mining, fishing, engineering, seem to have been male-dominated, the female voice has been repressed. However, a closer look soon reveals that in all these areas, as well as many others, women had an equally important place, and throughout Cornish history were eager to have their stories recorded in writing.

The large mass of anonymous broadsheet poems also merits renewed attention. In this editor's view at least, such poems were the 'real' material read by the working-class people of Cornwall and they reflect many of the people's interests and concerns. Indeed, it has to be acknowledged that the readership of the poets included here was fairly limited. However, while I have endeavoured to give a representative sample of these fascinating anonymous poems, any more would be unwieldy, not to mention depressing, for most treat very similar themes of mining disasters and shipwrecks along the Cornish coast. For the interested reader, there is a very fine collection of these broadsheets in the Courtney Library of the Royal Institution of Cornwall.[22]

This anthology, then, celebrates the whole range of Cornish poetry in English, the language so many Cornish writers claimed and shaped in their own way. It should be seen as complementary to *The Wheel*, Tim Saunders' recent anthology of poetry in Cornish,[23] thus enabling us to see through the medium of poetry a more complete picture of changing Cornish identity over five centuries.

Alan M. Kent,
Lanbrebois / Probus,
Kernow / Cornwall.

# References

1   Cited in A. K. Hamilton Jenkin (1925) 'Cornish Mines and Miners' in *Old Cornwall*, 1:1, p.13.

2   Cited in A. L. Rowse (1991 [1969]) *The Cornish in America*, Redruth: Dyllansow Truran, pp.255–256.

3   W. Herbert Thomas (1892) *Poems of Cornwall*, Penzance: F. Rodda, p.vii. For a useful exploration of 'West Barbary' see Bernard Deacon, 'The hollow jarring of the distant steam engines': Images of Cornwall between West Barbary and Delectable Duchy' in Ella Westland (ed.) (1997) *Cornwall: The Cultural Construction of Place*, Penzance: The Patten Press, pp.7–24.

4   W. H. Hudson (1981 [1908]) *The Land's End*, London: Wildwood House, pp.95–96.

5   Matthew Arnold (1867) *The Study of Celtic Literature*, London: Smith and Elder.

6   See L. E. Elliot-Binns (1955) *Medieval Cornwall*, London: Methuen.

7   See chapters by Paul Laity, Mark Stoyle, Isobel Harvey, Ian Arthurson and James Derriman in Simon Parker (ed.) (1998) *Cornwall Marches On!* Truro: Keskerdh Kernow, pp. 5–35

8   See Francis Rose-Troup (1913) *The Western Rebellions of 1549*, London: Smith, Elder and Co. p.221.

9   John Angarrack (1999) *Breaking the Chains: Censorship, Deception and the Manipulation of Public Opinion in Cornwall*, Camborne: Stannary Publications, pp.50–53.

10  For detail on these writers, see Alan M. Kent and Tim Saunders (eds.) (2000) *Looking at the Mermaid: A Reader in Cornish Literature 900–1900*, London: Francis Boutle.

11  See Amy Hale, 'Rethinking Celtic Cornwall: An Ethnographic Approach' and 'Genesis of the Celto-Cornish Revival: L.C. Duncombe-Jewell and the Cowethas Kelto-Kernuak' in Philip Payton (ed.) (1997) *Cornish Studies: Five*, Exeter: University of Exeter Press, pp. 85–99 and pp.100–111.

12  F. E. Halliday (ed.) (1953) *Richard Carew of Antony*, London: Andrew Melrose, pp. 303–308.

13  Thomas, *Op.cit.*

14  See H. J. Whitfeld (1852) *Scilly and its Legends*. London: Timpkin, Marshall and Co; William Bottrell, (ed.) (1870) *Traditions & Hearthside Stories of West Cornwall: First Series*. Penzance: W. Cornish, (ed.) (1873) *Traditions & Hearthside Stories of West Cornwall: Second Series*. Penzance: Beare and Son, (ed.) (1880) *Traditions & Hearthside Stories of West Cornwall: Third Series*. Penzance: F. Rodda.

15  Robert Morton Nance (1956) *The Cledry Plays: Drolls of Old Cornwall for Village Acting and Home Reading*, Penzance: The Federation of Old Cornwall Societies.

16  Christopher Morris (ed.) (1947) *Journeys of Celia Fiennes*. London: Cresset Press; Pat Rogers (ed.) (1971) *Daniel Defoe: A Tour Through the Whole Island of Great Britain [1724–1726]*, Harmondsworth: Penguin.

17  See Roger Jones (ed.) (1985) *John Skinner: The West Country Tour 1797*, Bradford on Avon: Ex Libris Press; Dinah Craik (1884) *An Unsentimental Journey through Cornwall*, London: Macmillan and Co; Chris Thomas. 'See Your Own Country First: The Geography of a Railway Landscape' in Westland, *Op.cit.*, pp.107–128.

18  See numerous examples in Richard Gendall (ed.) (1997) *A Practical Dictionary of Modern Cornish: Part One, Cornish-English*, Menheniot: Teere ha Tavaz.

19  For comment on this, see K. C. Phillipps (ed.) (1993) *A Glossary of the Cornish Dialect*, Padstow: Tabb House, pp.1–17.

20  See Simon Parker (1997) *A Star on the Mizzen*, Liskeard: Giss' On Books; Alan M. Kent (1998) *Dreaming in Cornish*, Liskeard: Giss' On Books.

21  Alan M. Kent (1998) *Wives, Mothers and Sisters: Feminism, Literature and Women Writers of Cornwall*, Penzance: The Patten Press.

22  The Sunley Collection of Broadsheets RIC, Truro, Cornwall. See for example: 'A Tragical Calamity! which occurred at West Wheal Grylls Mine, 1873' and Thomas Morris (n.d) 'Upwards of Twenty Lives Lost by Awful Shipwrecks, in Cornwall'.
23  Tim Saunders (ed.) (1999)*The Wheel, an anthology of modern poetry in Cornish 1850–1980*, London: Francis Boutle.

# The Poems

**Andrew Boorde c.1500–c.1560**

## Iche Cham a Cornyshe Man[1]

Iche cham a Cornyshe man, al che can brew;[2]
It wyll make one to kacke, also to spew;
It is dycke and smoky, and also it is dyn;
It is lyke wash, as pygges had wrestled dryn.
Iche cannot brew, nor dresse Fleshe, nor vyshe;
Many volke do segge, I mar many a good dyshe.
Dup the dore, gos! iche hab some dyng to seg,
"When olde knaues be dead, yonge knaues be fleg."
Iche chaym yll afyngred, iche swere by my fay
Iche nys not eate no soole sens yester daye;
Iche wolde fayne taale ons myd the cup;
Nym me a quart of ale, that iche may if of sup.
A, good gosse, iche hab a toome, vyshe, and also tyn;
Drynke, gosse, to me, or els iche chyl begyn.
God! watysh great colde, and fynger iche do abyd!
Wyl your bedauer, gosse, come home at the next tyde.
Iche pray God to coun him wel to vare,
That, whan he comit home, myd me he do not starre
For putting a straw dorow his great net.
Another pot of ale, good gosse, now me fet;
For my bedauer wyl to London, to try the law,
To sew Tre poll pen, for waggyng of a straw.
Now, gosse, farewell! yche can no lenger abyde;
Iche must ouer to the ale howse at the yender syde;
And now come myd me, gosse, I thee pray,
And let vs make merry, as long as we may.

### Nicholas Roscarrock c.1548–1634

## A Sonnet[1]

If this my labour serve but for a foyle
to lend a luster to some learned quill
to perfect this my undertaken toyle,
I have my wishe althoughe I want my will:
deprivde of helpe and destitude of skill,
whoe wholy in this work applied my penn
to honour God and not to humour men.
If he be pleas'd, I have my harts desyre,
wishing good mynds in doubt to deame the best,
and for my paines I seek noe better hyre
of such as are with scorne and spleene possest
but base contempt with which content I rest.
Believe well, & live well, & hope well for Bliss,
Farewell, & wish well, to him that wrote this.

## A Friendly Warning about Saints[2]

If men admyre the lives of these our saints,
muse not, for why they were for wonders written
by wise and learned, free from all attaints,
yea saints themselves and most unlike to fitten;
Which will be cause sufficient to content
The myndes of such as have no ill intent.

As for the rest, which sensuall, drown'd in sense,
so senseless are as nothing will believe
but self conceit and self wills false pretence,
It recks not much what Censure they do give,
for sunn and starrs they scarsely will esteeme
of greater circuitt then there sense dothe deeme.

What God can doe to make his power appeare
when it is done no wise man will denye,
If it be truely prov'de as it is here,
Except the wise be fooles and true men lye.
This maye suffice; if not it is noe wonder,
For saints and sinners will be still asunder.

# Of Saint Aaron[3]

Saint Aaron, fronted in the foremost place
of this my boke, by reason of thy name,
One of the Martyrs first of Brittish race
claiming as't weare in sort by right the same,
To thee on bended knees prayers I frame,
to thousand Mates, to all that doe insue,
Yea, to the holies all of Heavenly crue,

To poure fourth prayers unto the power divine,
I meane our God the Blessed one in three,
to bless me and this work well ment of myne,
and pardon faults which here committed bee
against my will, for no man all can see;
In hope whereof I will proceed to end
This toyle in hope good mindes the same will mend.

## Richard Carew 1555–1620

## Prosopopeia[1]

I crave not courteous aid of friends
  To blaze my praise in verse;
Nor, proud of vaunt, mine author's names
  In catalogue rehearse.

I of no willing wrong complain,
  Which force or stealth hath wrought,
No fruit I promise from the tree
  Which forth this blood hath brought.

I curry not with smoothing terms,
  Ne yet rude threats I blast:
I seek no patron for my faults,
  I plead no needless haste.

But, as a child of feeble force,
  I keep my father's home,
And, bashful at each stranger's sight,
  Dare not abroad to roam.

Save to his kin of nearest blood,
  Or friends of dearest price,
Who, for his sake, not my desert,
  With welcome me entice.


## The Well of St Keyne[2]

In name, in shape, in quality,
  The well is very quaint;
The name to lot of Keyne befell,
  No over-holy saint.
The shape – four trees of diverse kinds,
  Withy, oke, elme and ash,
Make with their roots an arched roofe,
  Whose floore this spring doth wash.
The quality – that man or wife,
  Whose chance or choice attaines,
First of the sacred stream to drinke,
  Thereby the mastry gaines.

# The River Lynher[3]

The storehouse of sun's chevisance,[4]
The clock whose measures time doth dance,
The moon's vassal, the lord of chance

                          Oceanus,[5]

Ere year's compass his circle end,
From hugy bosom, where they wend,
His scaly brood to greet doth send

                          His wife Tellus.[6]

Some sail but with the coasting shore,
Some multiply the harbour's store,
Some far into the river bore,

                          Amongst the rest.

A threefold rout, of Argus[7] hue,
Kind to increase, foes to eschew,
With Lynher's supple mantle blue

                          Themselves revest.

What time, enrich'd by Phoebus's[8] rays,
The alder his new wealth displays
Of budded groats, and welcome pays

                          Unto the spring,

The trouts of middle growth begin,
And equal peis'd 'twixt either fin,
At wonted host, Dan Lynher's inn,

                          Take their lodging.

Next, as the days up early rise,
In comes the peal, whose smaller size,
In his more store and oft supplies

                          A praise doth find.

Lastly, the salmon, king of fish,
Fills with good cheer the Christmas dish,
Teaching that season must relish

                          Each in his kind.

## Epitaph for John Arundell[9]

Seek not, blind eyes, the living with the dead,
'Tis earth you see: our Arundell is gone
To join with Christ, as member to his head,
And scorns and pities this our bootless moan.
   Yet pardon us, sweet soul: man's nature bears
   We to thy loss should sacrifice our tears.

Thou time has changed to eternity,
But timeless was that time in our regard,
Since nought thou leav'st us save the memory
Of thy dear worth, so soon not to be spar'd.
   Soft be the grave unto thy resting bones:
   Short be the date that us again atones.


## *From* A Herring's Tail[10]

This while Sir Lymazon the upmost story won,
And with soft haste to mount the middle spire began;
Step after step he slides, and length steals from his way,
Yet length he seems to add, swarving, but not astray;
For not direct he climbs, climbing direct may breed
More speed than ease, and more hazard of fall than speed.
Like as the gerfalcon, a point of height to win
Upon the waggling winged heron, doth not begin
His stairy mount upright, but elsewhere soareth out,
And turning tail, a winding compass sets about,
That eye fixt by desire, and wing guided by the eye,
And both not plied with more strength than industry,
May to a loftier pitch so make return in the end,
And with less sense of pain dazzling steepness ascend.
So our dew's son sometimes an hold most circles makes,
Now lines in angles sharp, now in obtuse he breaks,
There true love knots he twines, here paints some
    flowers or tree:
Uncouth the shapes, but bootful to his bent they be,
The circles to compass, the angles up to get,
The knots to bind, the trees and flowers a grace to set.
And whereso art or fortune taught or brought his ways,
A varnish on his footsteps smooth and bright he lays,
Smooth as the path, which under walking finger yields,
And twixt two hillocks leads unto th' Elysian fields:

Bright as the worm, whose tail the highway side bestars,
And on the helm for canvisado serves in wars.
And now by scale he shorten'd had the steep ascent,
And with glad eye laid holdfast on the battlement.


## Full Thirteen Five of Years[11]

Full thirteen five of years I toyling have o'erpast
  And in the fourteenth, weary entered am I at last.
While rocks, sands, stormes, and leaks, to take my bark away
  By grief, troubles, sorrows, sickness did essay.
And yet arrived I am not at the porth of death,
  The port to everlasting life that openeth.
My time uncertain, Lord! long certain cannot be,
  That best to mee's unknown, and only known to thee.
O! by repentance and amendment, grant that I
  May still live in thy fear – and in thy favour dye.

**Michael Drayton 1563–1631**

## *From* First Song, Poly-Olbion

The sprightly Muse her wing displays,
And the French islands first surveys;
Bears up with Neptune, and in glory
Transcends proud Cornwal's promontory;
There crowns Mount-Michael, and descries
How all those riverets fall and rise;
Then takes in Tamer, as she bounds
The Cornish and Devonian grounds.
And whilst the Dev'nshire nymphs relate
Their loves, their fortunes, and estate,
Dert undertaketh to revive
Our Brute,[1] and sings his first arrive:
Then northward to the verge she bends,
And at her first song at Ax she ends.

.............................................................

Ye sacred bards, that to your harps' melodious strings
Sung th' ancient Heroes' deeds (the monuments of Kings)
And in your dreadful verse ingrav'd the prophecies,
The aged word's descent and genealogies;
If, as those Druids taught, which kept the British rites,
And dwelt in darksome groves, there counselling with sprites
(But their opinions fail'd, by error led awry,
As since clear truth hath shew'd to their posterity)
When these our souls by death our bodies do forsake,
They instantly again do other bodies take;
I could have wisht your spirits redoubled in my breast,
To give my verse applause to time's eternal rest.
Thus scarcely said the Muse, but hovering while she hung
Upon the Celtic wastes, the sea-nymphs loudly sung:
'Ye happy islands set within the British seas,

.............................................................

With shrill and jocund shouts, th' immeasur'd deeps awake,
And let the Gods of sea their secret bowr's forsake,
Whilst our industrious muse Great Britain forth shall bring,
Crown'd with those glorious wreaths that beautify the spring;
And whilst green Thetis'[2] nymphs, with many an amorous lay
Sing our invention safe unto her long-wisht bay.'
Upon the utmost end of Cornwal's furrowing beak,
Where Bresan[3] from the land the tilting waves doth break;
The shore let her transcend, the promont to descry,
And view about the point th' unnumbred fowl that fly;
Some rising like a storm from off the troubled sand,

Seem in their hov'ring flight to shadow all the land;
Some sitting on the beach to prune their painted breasts,
As if both earth and air they only did possess;
Whence climbing to the cliffs, herself she firmly sets
The bourns, the brooks, the becks, the rills, the rivulets,
Exactly to derive; receiving in her way
That streightened tongue of land, where at Mount-Michael's bay,
Rude Neptune cutting in, a cantle forth doth take;
And on the other side, Hayle's vaster mouth doth make
A chersonese[4] thereof, the corner clipping in;
Where to th' industrious Muse the Mount doth thus begin:
'Before thou further pass, and leave this setting shore,
Whose towns unto the saints that lived here of yore
(Their fasting, works and pray'rs, remaining to our shames)
Were rear'd, and justly call'd by their peculiar names,
The builders honour still; this due and let them have,
As deign to drop a tear upon each holy grave;
Whose charity and zeal, instead of knowledge stood:
For surely in themselves they were right simply good.
If credulous too much, thereby th' offended heaven,
In their devout intents yet be their sins forgiven.'
Then from his rugged tops the tears down trickling fell;
And in his passion stirr'd, again began to tell
Strange things, that in his days time's course had brought to pass:
That forty miles now sea, sometimes fine fore-land was;
And that a forest then, which now with him is flood,
Whereof he first was call'd the Hoar-rock in the wood;[5]
Relating then how long this soil had laid forlorn,
As that her Genius now had almost her forsworn,
And of their ancient love did utterly repent,
Sith to destroy herself that fatal tool she lent,
To which th' insatiate slave her intrails out doth draw,
That thrusts his gripple hand into her golden maw;
And for his part doth wish, that it were in his pow'r
To let the ocean in, her wholly to devour.

................................................................................

When chore doth call her on, that wholly doth betake
Herself unto the Loo;[6] transform'd into a lake,
Through that impatient love she had to entertain
The lustful Neptune oft; whom when his wracks restrain,
Impatient of the wrong, impetuously he raves:
And in his rageful flow, the furious King of waves
Breaks foaming o'er the beach, whom nothing seems to cool,
Till he have wrought his will on that capacious pool;
Where Menedge,[7] by his brooks, a chersonese is cast,
Widening the slender shore to ease it in the waste;
A promont jutting out into the dropping south,

That with his threatning cliffs in horrid Neptune's mouth,
Derides him and his pow'r: nor cares how him he greets.
Next Roseland[8] (as his friend, the mightier Menedge) meets
Great Neptune when he swells, and rageth at the rocks
(Set out into those seas) inforcing through his shocks
Those arms of sea that thrust into the tinny strand,
By their meandred creeks indenting of that land,
Whose fame by every tongue is for her minerals hurl'd,
Near from the mid-day's point, thro' out the western world.
Here Vale a lively flood, her nobler name that gives
To Falmouth; and by whom it famous ever lives,
Whose entrance is from sea so intricately wound,
Her haven angled so about her harb'rous sound,
That in her quiet bay a hundred ships may ride
Yet not the tallest mast be of the tall'st descry'd;
Her bravery to this nymph when neighbouring rivers told,
Her mind to them again she briefly doth unfold:
'Let Camel of her course and curious windings boast,
In that her greatness reigns sole mistress of that coast
'Twixt Tamer and that bay, where Hayle pours fourth her pride,
And let us (nobler nymphs) upon her mid-day side
Be frolic with the best. Thou Foy, before us all,
By thine own named town made famous in thy fall,
As Low amongst us here; a most delicious brook,
With all our sister nymphs, that to the noonsted look,
Which gliding from the hills, upon the tinny ore,
Betwixt your high-rear'd banks, resort to this our shore;
Lov'd streams, let us exult, and think ourselves no less
Than those upon their side, the setting that possess.'
    Which Camel over-heard: but what doth she respect
Their taunts, her proper course that loosely doth neglect?
As frantic, ever since her British Arthur's blood,
By Mordred's murtherous hand was mingled with her flood.
For as that river best might boast that conqueror's breath,
So sadly she bemoans his too untimely death;
Who after twelve proud fields against the Saxon fought,
Yet back unto her banks by fate was lastly brought:
As though no other place on Britain's spacious earth
Were worthy of his end, but where he had his birth.

**Sidney Godolphin 1610–1643**

# Meditation on the Nativity

Lord, when the wise men came from far,
Led to thy cradle by a star,
Then did the shepherds too rejoice,
Instructed by thy angel's voice;
Blest were the wise men in their skill,
And shepherds in their harmless will.

Wise men in tracing nature's laws
Ascend unto the highest cause;
Shepherds with humble fearfulness
Walk safely, though their light be less:
Though wise men better know the way,
It seems no honest heart can stray.

There is no merit in the wise
But love (the shepherd's sacrifice):
Wise men, all ways of knowledge past,
To th' shepherds' wonder come at last;
To know can only wonder breed,
And not to know is wonder's seed.

A wise man at the altar bows
And offers up his studied vows,
And is received; may not the tears,
Which spring too from a shepherd's fears,
And sighs upon his frailty spent,
Though not distinct, be eloquent?

'Tis true, the object sanctifies
All passions which within us rise,
But since no creature comprehends
The cause of causes, end of ends,
He who himself vouchsafes to know
Best pleases his creator so.

When then our sorrows we apply
To our own wants and poverty,
When we look up in all distress
And our own misery confess,
Sending both thanks and prayers above:
Then, though we do not know, we love.

# Song

Or love me less, or love me more
  And play not with my liberty;
Either take all, or all restore;
  Bind me at least, or set me free;
Let me some nobler torture find
  Than of a doubtful wavering mind:
Take all my peace; but you betray
  Mine honour too this cruel way.

'Tis true that I have nursed before
  That hope of which I now complain,
And, having little, sought no more,
  Fearing to meet with your disdain:
The sparks of favour you did give,
  I gently blew to make them live;
And yet have gained by all this care
  No rest in hope, nor in despair.

I see you wear that pitying smile
  Which you have still vouchsafed my smart,
Content thus cheaply to beguile
  And entertain a harmless heart;
But I no longer can give way
  To hope, which doth so little pay,
And yet I dare no freedom owe
  Whilst you are kind, though but in show.

Then give me more, or give me less,
  Do not disdain a mutual sense,
Or your unpitying beauties dress
  In their own free indifference.
But show not a severer eye,
  Sooner to give me liberty;
For I shall love the very scorn
  Which for my sake you do put on.

# Constancy

Love unreturned howe'er the flame
Seem great and pure, may still admit
Degrees of more, and a new name
And strength acceptance gives to it.

Till then, by honour there's no tie
Laid on it, that it ne'er decay;
The mind's last act by constancy
Ought to be sealed, and not the way.

Did aught but love's perfection bind
Who should assign at what degree
Of love, faith ought to fix the mind,
And in what limits we are free.

So hardly in a single heart
Is any love conceived,
That fancy still supplies one part,
Supposing it received.

When undeceived, such love retires,
'Tis but a model lost:
A draught of what might be expires,
Built but at fancy's cost.

Yet if the ruin one tear move,
From pity, not love, sent,
Though not a palace, it will prove
The most wished monument.


## Fair Friend, 'Tis True your Beauties Move

Fair friend, 'tis true your beauties move
    My heart to a respect,
Too little to be paid with love,
    Too great for your neglect.

I neither love nor yet am free,
    For though the flame I find
Be not intense in the degree
    'Tis of the purest kind.

It wants of love, but pain:
    Your beauty takes my sense;
And lest you should that price disdain,
    My thoughts, too, feel the influence.

'Tis not a passion's first access
    Ready to multiply,
But like love's calmest state it is
    Possessed with victory.

It is like love to truth reduced,
  All the false values gone,
Which were created and induced
  By fond imagination.

'Tis either fancy or 'tis fate
  To love you more than I:
I love you at your beauty's rate;
  Less were an injury.

Like unstamped gold, I weigh each grace,
  So that you may collect
The intrinsic value of your face
  Safely from my respect.

And this respect would merit love,
  Were not so fair a sight
Payment enough: for who dare move
  Reward for his delight?

## On Sir F. Carew

No way unworthy of his fair descent,
Careless of that brave life which we lament
All the good ends of living here acquired
Much loved, much honoured, and how much desired
His virtue past all trials shining far
Bright in the brightest sphere of fame, the war;
Submitting gladly to that fate, which oft
He hath so boldly, and so bravely sought,
Here Carew lies, but, Reader, may that name
Not move thy tears, but warm thee with like flame.

# Constant Love

'Tis affection but dissembled,
  Or dissembled liberty,
To pretend thy passion changed
  With changes of thy mistress' eye,
  Following her inconstancy.

Hopes which do from favour flourish
  May perhaps as soon expire
As the cause which did them nourish,
  And disdained they may retire;
  But love is another fire.

For if beauty cause thy passion;
  In a fair, resistless eye
Melt thee with its soft expression –
  Then thy hopes will never die,
  Nor be cured by cruelty.

'Tis not scorn that can remove thee;
  For thou either wilt not see
Such loved beauty not to love thee,
  Or wilt else consent that she
  Judge not as she ought of thee.

Thus thou either canst not sever
  Hope from what appears so fair,
Or unhappier thou canst never
  Find contentment in despair,
  Nor make love a trifling care.

There are see but few retiring
  Steps in all the paths of love,
Made by such who in aspiring
  Meeting scorn their hearts remove;
  Yet e'en those ne'er change their love.

**Thomas Hogg 1777–1835**

## Godolphin[1]

Glows not each Cornish bosom at the name
Of brave Godolphin with a patriot's flame?

Relate, O Muse! how once his victor band
With Spanish gore distain'd the humid strand.
  Sweet morn arose and chas'd the shades of night;
The heath-clad hills were tipp'd with golden light;
Ungurth'd the fiery steeds enjoyed in the hall;
When, white with dust, upon a horse of foam,
A breathless herald reach'd his ancient dome.

Anxious to hear the tidings that he bore,
Godolphin quick unbarred the massive door.
'Most valiant knight!' he said, 'a hostile train,
In painted vessels, plow the southern main;
St Michael's banner waves, conspicuous far,
And bids me hasten to announce the war!'

  Down many a dewy vale, on zephyrs borne,
Shrill blasts flew, echoing, from Godolphin's horn.
The martial race the sounds no sooner hear,
Than seizes each his bow and glittering spear.
Along the avenues they speed their way;
Ranks close on ranks, and form in bright array.

The chieftain then: 'My friends! a hostile train,
In painted vessels, plows the southern main;
St Michael's banner waves, conspicuous far,
And bids us hasten to repel the war.
Ne'er be it said old Cornwall fear'd a blow,
Whilst, listless, we declin'd to meet the foe!'

  Up the brown hill, array'd in radiant pride,
With dauntless minds, now all the warriors ride;
The summit gain'd, Godolphin's rapid view
O'er sea and land, o'er town and cottage flew.
Beyond St Michael's towers the darken'd skies
Show where thick clouds from burning hamlets rise.

A thirst for glory every bosom fills;
As arrows swift, they fly adown the hills;
From amidst the dust that hovers o'er their way,
Their glitt'ring arms emit a transient ray.

Meanwhile, the foe pursue their fierce career,
And on St Paul's high tower their standard rear;
Then march, relentless, down the steep hill-side
To where calm Mousehole overlooks the tide.
They it, alas! doom to destructive fires;
The wreathing smoke from different parts aspires;
Th' affrighted victims of their wrath deplore
Their mournful fate along the desert shore;
With shrieks shrieks mingle as their dwellings burn,
And the sad sounds the sorrowing waves return.
On, brave Godolphin! Soon Penzance must fall.
See! they approach, with thundering tread, her wall.

Through Marghasiowe he pursues his way,
To try the fortune of th' eventful day.
The foaming steeds, impatient for the war,
Surpass the winds, and smell it from afar.
The castle-archers on the ramparts stand;
Their acclamations run along the strand.

On, brave Godolphin! O'er the verge of fate
Penzance now hangs; the foes are at her gate.
Soon through her streets the snorting horses prance,
And every yeoman aims his mortal lance;
'The forlorn hope,' sent on the town to fire,
From their approach like timid deer retire;
Th' unerring archers scatter death around;
And foes o'er foes fall gasping on the ground,
With dying groans; and with the horrid clang
Of clashing arms thy shores, old Ocean, rang.
Hot was the conflict; o'er the yellow strand
The barbarous crew fled from the patriot band;
Such as escap'd to tell the fatal tale
Sought refuge in their ships, and quickly hoisted sail.

The victor-hero by the azure flood,
Hail'd with loud shouts of joy, triumphant stood;
St. Michael's bells full merrily were rung;
While he became the theme of every tongue.
Their children fathers still exulting tell,
How brave Godolphin fought, and how the Spaniards fell.

# Witchcraft[2]

The frith of deep Solinus laves
Dread threshold of fell witchcraft's caves;
Within Tolpedon's[3] airy view,
Their orgies, now, the hag's pursue;
And, in their midnight cell intent,
Sap ocean's vaulted firmament;
Ingredients in the cauldron throw,
Of Cornwall's Star to damp the glow.
   "What," one sister asks, "expects
He? prowls he seeking lost effects?"
   "No; he ransacks Silura's[4] domes,
For Tyrian manuscripts and tomes:
Our grand-dames, nobly, formed that tide;
Bade navies o'er sunk castles ride;
Let loose the winds with lawless sweep;
Whelmed forests, churches, in the deep;
Destruction, drove, with flowing reins,
O'er Lionesse and all her plains;
Their spells, – by us long sought in vain,
May meet his search below the main."
   Then the elder weird, "If such his aim,
I'll drown him, or consume with flame;
Through nature all, his empire own,
Nor twinkle one star before his frown."
   In night she plunged, resolved to foil
The antiquarian's anxious toil.
He, disobedient to the nymph,
Had strayed far in a lake of lymph:
A wonderous space, where, uncontroll'd,
The waves, distilled, of ocean, roll'd;
As Whitaker[5] relates, " nor land,
Nor waters, round his way, expand,
Nor liquid air; of each composed,
Th' enchanted medium interposed."
   Before him towers and pillars lay;
Triumphal arches, sculptured, grey;
The vestige of squares thrown down
Bespoke the court-end of a town.
   "Alas!" said he, "these ruins lie,
Inspiring deep soliloquy;
To mind, each scattered fragment brings
Mutations of terrestrial things.
Ye consecrated domes of faith,
Where piety's ambrosial breath,
Symphonies, rose in columns rich,

Round every god, in every niche.
Ye halls of eloquence, which rung
With speeches in old Cornwall's tongue;
Ye palaces, and princely walls,
Where levees thronged; assembled balls

..........................................................

The dazzling pomp of triumph fled,
On canvas may the wrecks be spread:
Wealth, banquets, beauty, deluged saints,
Your fame a lasting moral paints.


## Fairies

As Christian light, the land, pervades,
The ancient faith, retiring, fades.
Divinities, whom Greece, – whom Rome,
Had worshipped in the marble dome,
Degraded, sink. Some lurking seed,
Prolific, of the Druid creed,
Lay scattered round; – and oft, would blow,
Luxuriant weeds, o'er flowers below.
Those streams, which flowed to purify,
Took, from the soil, a tincturing dye.
Credulity, in witchcraft's cell,
With magic, shunned the day, to dwell;
At the period, we now write,
In fairies, Britain found delight.
More numerous than the Saxon arms,
In Cornwall sprang enchantment's charms.
On moonlight heath, or dewy green,
By Fancy's eye, their troops were seen:
Their gambols, by the midnight stream,
And dance in Cynthia's silver beam;
The circles, formed, where arms had rung,
Were themes which to the harp were sung.

**Humphry Davy 1778–1829**

# In Ludgvan Churchyard[1]

My eye is wet with tears
For I see the white stones
    That are covered with names
    The stones of my forefather's graves

No grass grows upon them
For deep in the earth
    In darkness and silence the organs of life
    To their primitive atoms return

Through ages the air
Has been moist with their blood
Through ages the seeds of
    The thistle has fed
    On what was once motion and form

The white land that floats
Through the heavens
Is pregnant with
    That which was life
And the moonbeams
    That whiten it came
From the breath and spirit of man.

Thoughts roll not beneath the dust
No feeling is in the cold grave.
Neither thought nor feeling can die
They have leaped to other worlds
They are far above the skies

They kindle in the stars
They dance in the light of suns
Or they live in the comet's white haze

These poor remains of frame
Were the source of the organs of flesh
That feel the control of my will
That are active and mighty in me.

They gave to my body form
Is nought in your dying limbs
That gave to my spirit life
The blood that rolled through their veins

Was the germ of my bodily power
Their spirit gave me no germ
        Of kindling energy


# The Sons of Genius[2]

Bright bursting through the awful veil of night
        The lunar beams upon the ocean play;
The watery billows shine with trembling light,
        Where the swift breezes skim along the sea.

The glimmering stars in yon ethereal plain
        Grow pale, and fade before the lurid beams,
Save where fair Venus, shining o'er the main,
        Conspicuous still with fainter radiance gleams.

Clear as the azure firmament above,
        Save where the white cloud floats upon the breeze;
All tranquil is the bosom of the grove,
        Save where the zephyr warbles through the trees.

Now the poor shepherd wandering to his home,
        Surveys the darkening scene with fearful eye,
On every green sees little elfins roam,
        And haggard sprites along the moonbeams fly.

While superstition rules the vulgar soul,
        Forbids the energies of man to rise,
Raised far above her low, her mean control,
        Aspiring genius seeks her native skies.

She loves the silent, solitary hours;
        She loves the stillness of the starry night,
When o'er the bright'ning view Selene pours
        The soft effulgence of her pensive light.

'Tis then, disturb'd not by the glare of day,
        To mild tranquillity alone resign'd,
Reason extends her animating sway
        O'er the calm empire of the peaceful mind.

Before her lucid, all-enlightening ray,
        The pallid spectres of the night retire;
She drives the gloomy terrors far away,
        And fills the bosom with celestial fire.

46

Inspired by her, the sons of genius rise
    Above all earthly thoughts, all vulgar care;
Wealth, power, and grandeur, they alike despise, –
    Enraptured by the good, the great, the fair.

A thousand varying joys to them belong, –
    The charms of nature and her changeful scenes:
Theirs is the music of the vernal song,
    And theirs the colours of the vernal plains.

Theirs is the purple-tinged evening ray,
    With all the radiance of the evening sky;
Theirs is the splendour of the risen day,
    Enshrined in glory by the sun's bright eye.

For them the zephyr fans the odorous dale;
    For them the warbling streamlet softly flows;
For them the Dryads shade the verdant vale;
    For them sweet Philomel attunes her woes.

To them no wakeful moonbeam shines in vain
    On the dark bosom of the trackless wood;
Sheds its mild radiance o'er the desert plain,
    Or softly glides along the crystal flood.

Yet not alone delight the soft and fair,
    Alike the grander scenes of nature move;
Yet not alone her beauties claim their care,
    The great, sublime, and terrible they love.

The sons of nature, – they alike delight
    In the rough precipice's broken steep;
In the bleak terrors of the stormy night;
    And in the thunders of the threatening deep.

When the red lightnings through the ether fly,
    And the white foaming billows lash the shores;
When to the rattling thunders of the sky
    The angry demon of the waters roars;

And when, untouch'd by Nature's living fires,
    No native rapture fills the drowsy soul;
Then former ages, with their tuneful lyres,
    Can bid the fury of the passions fall.

By the blue taper's melancholy light,
    Whilst all around the midnight torrents pour,

And awful glooms beset the face of night,
    They wear the silent, solitary hour.

Ah! then how sweet to pass the night away
    In silent converse with the Grecian page,
Whilst Homer tunes his ever-living lay,
    Or reason listens to the Athenian sage.

To scan the laws of Nature, to explore
    The tranquil reign of mild Philosophy;
Or on Newtonian wings sublime to soar
    Through the bright regions of the starry sky.

Ah! who can paint what raptures fill the soul
    When Attic freedom rises to the war,
Bids the loud thunders of the battle roll,
    And drives the tyrant trembling from her shore?

From these pursuits the sons of genius scan
    The end of their creation, – hence they know
The fair, sublime, immortal hopes of man,
    From whence alone undying pleasures flow.

By science calmed, over the peaceful soul,
    Bright with eternal Wisdom's lucid ray,
Peace, meek of eye, extends her soft control,
    And drives the puny Passions far away.

Virtue, the daughter of the skies supreme,
    Directs their life, informs their glowing lays;
A steady friend, her animating beam,
    Sheds its soft lustre o'er their latter days.

When life's warm fountains feel the frost of time,
    When the cold dews of darkness close their eyes,
She shows the parting soul upraised, sublime,
    The brighter glories of her kindred skies.

Thus the pale moon, whose pure celestial light
    Has chased the gloomy clouds of heaven away,
Rests her white cheek, with silver radiance bright,
    On the soft bosom of the western sea.

Lost in the glowing wave, her radiance dies;
    Yet, while she sinks, she points her lingering ray
To the bright azure of the orient skies,
    To the fair dawning of the glorious day.

Like the tumultuous billows of the sea
    Succeed the generations of mankind;
Some in oblivious silence pass away,
    And leave not vestige of their lives behind.

Others, like those proud waves which beat the shore,
    A loud and momentary murmur raise;
But soon their transient glories are no more,
    No future ages echo with their praise.

Like yon proud rock, amidst the sea of time,
    Superior, scorning all the billow's rage,
The living sons of genius stand sublime,
    The immortal children of another age.

For those exist whose pure ethereal minds,
    Imbibing portions of celestial day,
Scorn all terrestrial cares, all mean designs,
    As bright-eyed eagles scorn the lunar ray.

Theirs is the glory of a lasting name,
    The meed of genius, and her living fire;
Theirs is the laurel of eternal fame,
    And theirs the sweetness of the muses lyre.

## Ode to Saint Michael's Mount

The sober eve with purple bright
Sheds o'er the hills her tranquil light
  In many a lingering ray;
The radiance trembles on the deep,
Where rises rough thy rugged steep,
  Old Michael, from the sea.

Around thy base, in azure pride,
Flows the silver-crested tide,
  In gently winding waves;
The Zephyr creeps thy cliffs around, –
Thy cliffs, with whispering ivy crown'd,
  And murmurs in thy caves.

Majestic steep! Ah, yet I love,
With many a lingering step, to rove
  Thy ivied rocks among;
Thy ivied, wave-beat rocks recall
The former pleasures of my soul,
  When life was gay and young.

Enthusiasm, Nature's child,
Here sung to me her wood-songs wild,
    All warm with native fire;
I felt her soul-awakening flame,
It bade my bosom burn for fame, –
    It bade me strike the lyre.

Soft as morning sheds her light
Through the dark azure of the Night
    Along the tranquil sea;
So soft the bright-eyed Fancy shed
Her rapturing dreams around my head,
    And drove my cares away.

When the white Moon with glory crown'd,
The azure of the sky around;
    Her silver radiance shed;
When shone the waves with trembling light,
And slept the lustre palely bright
    Upon the tower-clad head;

Then beauty bade my pleasure flow, –
Then beauty bade my bosom glow,
With mild and gentle fire!
    Then Mirth, and Cheerfulness, and Love,
Around my soul were wont to move,
    And thrill'd upon my lyre.

But when the Demon of the deep
Howl'd around thy rocky steep,
    And bade the tempests rise, –
Bade the white foaming billows roar,
And murmuring dash the rocky shore,
    And mingle with the skies;

Ah, then my soul was raised on high,
And felt the glow of ecstasy,
    And great emotions fill'd;
Then Joy and Terror reign'd by turns,
And now with Love the bosom burns,
    And now by Fear is chill'd.

Thus to the sweetest dreams resign'd,
The fairy Fancy ruled my mind,
    And shone upon my youth;
But now, to awful Reason given,
I leave her dear ideal heaven
    To hear the voice of Truth.

She claims my best, my loftiest song,
She leads a brighter maid along –
  Divine Philosophy,
Who bids the mounting soul assume
Immortal Wisdom's eagle plume,
  And penetrating eye,

Above Delusion's dusky maze,
Above deceitful Fancy's ways,
  With roses clad to rise;
To view a gleam of purest light
Bursting through Nature's misty night, –
  The radiance of the skies.


## The Tempest

The Tempest has darkened the face of the skies,
  The winds whistle wildly across the waste plain,
The Fiends of the whirlwind terrific arise,
  And mingle the clouds with the white-foaming main.

All dark is the night, and all gloomy the shore,
  Save when the red lightnings the ether divide,
Then follows the thunder with loud-sounding roar,
  And echoes in concert the billowy tide.

But though now all is murky and shaded with gloom,
  Hope, the soother, soft whispers the tempests shall cease;
Then Nature again in her beauty shall bloom,
  And enamour'd embrace the fair sweet-smiling Peace;

For the bright-blushing morning, all rosy with light,
  Shall convey on her wings the Creator of day;
He shall drive all the tempests and terrors of night,
  And Nature enliven'd, again shall be gay.

Then the warblers of Spring shall attune the soft lay,
  And again the bright flow'ret shall blush in the vale;
On the breast of the Ocean the Zephyr shall play,
  And the sunbeam shall sleep on the hill and the dale.

If the tempests of Nature so soon sink to rest –
  If her once-faded beauties so soon glow again,
Shall man be for ever by tempests oppress'd,
  By the tempests of passion, of sorrow, and pain?

Ah, no! for his passions and sorrow shall cease
  When the troublesome fever of life shall be o'er;
In the night of the grave he shall slumber in peace,
  And passion and sorrow shall vex him no more.

And shall not this night and its long dismal gloom,
  Like the night of the tempest, again pass away?
Yes! the dust of the earth in bright beauty shall bloom,
  And rise to the morning of heavenly day!

## Mount's Bay

Mild blows the Zephyr o'er the Ocean dark,
The Zephyr wafting the grey twilight clouds
Across the waves, to drink the solar rays
And blush with purple.
              By the orient gleam
Whitening the foam of the blue wave that breaks
Around his granite feet, but dimly seen,
Majestic Michael rises. He whose brow
Is crown'd with castles, and whose rocky sides
Are clad with dusky ivy: he whose base,
Beat by the storm of ages, stand unmoved
Amidst the wreck of things, the change of time.
That base encircled by the azure waves
Was once with verdure clad: the tow'ring oaks
There waved their branches green, – the sacred oaks
Whose awful shades among, the Druids stray'd
To cut the hallow'd mistletoe, and hold
High Converse with their Gods.
           On yon rough crag,
Where the wild Tamarisk whistle to the sea blast,
The Druid's harp was heard, swept by the breeze
To softest music, or to grander tones
Awaken'd by the awful master's hand.
Those tones shall sound no more! the rushing waves,
Raised from the vast Atlantic, have o'erwhelmed
The sacred groves. And deep the Druids lie
In the dark mist-clad sea of former time.
Ages had pass'd away, the stony altar
Was white with moss, when on its rugged base
Dire superstition raised the gothic fane,
And monks and priests existed.
           On the sea
The sunbeams tremble; and the purple light
Illumes the dark Bolerium,[3] seat of storms.
High are his granite rocks. His frowning brow

Hangs o'er the smiling Ocean. In his caves,
Th' Atlantic breezes murmur. In his caves,
Where sleep the haggard Spirits of the storm,
Wild dreary are the schistine rocks around
Encircled by the wave, where to the breeze
The haggard Cormorant shrieks. And far beyond
Are seen the cloud-like Islands, grey in mists.

Thy awful height, Bolerium, is not loved
By busy Man, and no one wanders there
Save he who follows Nature, – he who seeks
Amidst thy crags and storm-beat rocks to find
The marks of changes teaching the great laws
That raised the globe from chaos; or he whose soul
Is warm with fire poetic, – he who feels
When Nature smiles in beauty, or sublime
Rises in majesty, – he who can stand
Unawed upon thy summit, clad in tempests
And view with raptured mind the roaring deep
Rise o'er thy foam-clad base, while the black cloud
Bursts with the fire of Heaven –
                              He whose heart
Is warm with love and mercy, – he whose eye
Drops the bright tear when anxious Fancy paints
Upon his mind the image of the Maid,
The blue-eyed Maid who died beneath thy surge.
Where yon dark cliff o'ershadows the blue main,
Theora[4] died amidst the stormy waves,
And on its feet the sea-dews washed her corpse,
And the wild breath of storms shook her black locks.
Young was Theora; bluer was her eye
Than the bright azure of the moonlight night;
Fair was her cheek as is the ocean cloud
Red with the morning ray.
                              Amidst the groves,
And greens, and nodding rocks that overhang
The grey Killarney, pass'd her morning days
Bright with the beams of joy.
                              To solitude,
To Nature, and to God, she gave her youth;
Hence were her passions tuned to harmony.
Her azure eye oft glisten'd with the tear
Of sensibility, and her soft cheek
Glow'd with the blush of rapture. Hence, she loved
To wander 'midst the green-wood, silver'd o'er
By the bright moonbeam. Hence, she loved the rocks
Crown'd with nodding ivy, and the lake
Fair with the purple morning, and the sea

Expansive mingling with the arched sky.
Kindled by Genius, in her bosom glow'd
The sacred fire of Freedom. Hence, she scorn'd
The narrow laws of custom that control
Her feeble sex. Great in her energies,
She roam'd the fields of Nature, scann'd the laws
That move the ruling atoms, changing still,
Still rising into life. Her eagle eye,
Piercing the blue immensity of space,
Held converse with the lucid sons of Heaven,
The day-stars of creation, or pursued
The dusky planets rolling round the Sun
And drinking in his radiance light and life.
Such was the Maiden! Such was she who fled
Her native shores.
                         Dark in the midnight cloud,
When the wild blast upon its pinions bore
The dying shrieks of Erin's injured sons,
She 'scaped the murderer's arm.
                         The British bark
Bore her across the ocean. From the West
The whirlwind rose, the fire-fraught clouds of Heaven
Were mingled with the wave. The shatter'd bark
Sunk at thy feet, Bolerium, and the white surge
Closed on green Erin's daughter.


# The Song of Pleasure

The genial influence of the day
Had chased the lingering cold away;
Borne upon the Zephyr's wing,
Sweetly smiled the radiant Spring:
Her mild re-animating breath
Wakes Nature from her wintry death;
Attended by the laughing Hours,
She rises clad in flowers,
And lightly as she trips along,
The vernal warblers raise the song.
Rich in a thousand radiant dyes,
Around her steps the flow'rets rise,
The Zephyr sports, the sunbeams sleep
On the blue bosom of the deep.
And now, within my throbbing breast
I feel the influence of the Spring,
To ecstasy I tune my string,
And garlanded with odorous flowers,

I hasted to the shady grove,
I hasted to the roseate bowers
Where Pleasure dwells with Love.

There Youth, and Love, and Beauty, bound
The glowing rose my harp around;
Then to the daughter of Desire,
To bright-eyed Pleasure gave the lyre:
    She tuned the string
And smiling softer than the rosy sea,
When the young Morning blushes on her breast,
She raised the raptured lay,
    I heard her sing,
The song lull'd every care and every thought to rest.

Sons of Nature, hither haste,
The blessings of existence taste;
Listen to my friendly lay,
And your cares shall fly away,
Quick as fly the wintry snows
When the vernal Zephyr blows.
Let others, courting war's alarms,
Seek the bloody field of arms;
Let others, with undaunted soul,
Bid Bellona's thunders roll;
From the lightnings of their eye
Let the trembling squadrons fly;
Sons of Nature, you shall prove
A softer fight, the fight of love.
While you in soft repose are laid
Underneath the myrtle shade,
Amid the murky glooms of Death,
The sons of battle pant for breath.

Let the philosophic sage,
His silver tresses white with age,
Amid the chilling midnight damp,
Waste the solitary lamp,
To scan the laws of Nature o'er,
The paths of Science to explore;
Curb'd beneath his harsh control
The blissful Passions fly the soul.
You, the gentler sons of joy,
Softer studies shall employ!
He to curb the Passions tries,
You shall bid them all arise;
His want he wishes to destroy,
You shall all your wants enjoy.

Let the laurel, Virtue's meed,
Crown his age-besilver'd head,
The verdant laurel ever grows
Amid the sullen Winter's snows;
Let the rose, the flower of bliss,
The soft unwrinkled temples kiss;
Fann'd by the Zephyr's balmy wing,
The odorous rose adorns the Spring.

Let the Patriot die, to raise
A lasting monument of praise.
Ah, fool, to tear the glowing rose
From the mirth-encircled brows,
That around his dusky tomb
The ever-verdant bay may bloom!

Let Ambition's sons alone
Bow around the tottering throne,
Fly at Glory's splendid rays,
And, moth-like, die amidst a blaze;
You shall bow, and bow alone,
Before delicious Beauty's throne.
Lo! Theora treads the green,
All breathing grace and harmony she moves,
Fair as the mother of the Loves.
In graceful ringlets floats her golden hair;
From the bright azure of her eye
Expression's liquid lightnings fly.
Her cheek is fair.
Fair as the lily, when at dawning day,
Tinged with the morning's bright and purple ray,
Yonder scented groves among
She will listen to your song.

In yonder bower where roses bloom
Where the myrtle breathes perfume,
You shall at your ease recline,
And sip the soul-enlivening wine;
There the lyre, with melting lay,
Shall bid the soul dissolve away.
Soft as the Morning sheds her purple light
Through the dark azure of the Night,
So soft the God of slumber sheds
His roseate dews around your heads.

Such the blessings I bestow!
Haste, my sons, these blessings know!
Behold the flow'rets of the spring,

They wanton in the Zephyr's wing,
They drink the matin ether blue,
They sip the fragrant evening dew.
Man is but a short-lived flower,
His bloom but for a changeful hour!
Pass a little time away,
The rosy cheek is turn'd to clay:
No living joys, no transport's burn
In the dark sepulchral urn,
No Laurels crown the fleshless brows,
They fade together with the Rose.

## George Woodley 1786–1846

# Ode to Cornubia[1]

Genius of Cornwall! from thy deep-hewn caves,
  (Dank with the droppings of innum'rous mines,)
Where lull'd amidst the beat of troublous waves,
  In dread repose, pale Terror's brow reclines.

Or whether thou delight'st to sit sublime
  On Hensb'rough's[2] giant-peak, and thence survey
Each ragged monument of elder time, –
  The rude-wrought cromlech, cairn or burrow grey:

Or, like the eagle, rock'd amidst the storm,
  Lov'st thou that lofty pile, which, from the deep
Rising abrupt, in grandeur's wildest form,
  Waves high its quiv'ring crown o'er masses steep?

Or if th' impressive, wide-expanding gloom
  Of yonder ivied fortress please thee more; –
Where Meditation summons from the tomb
  Th' illustrious band who graced thy field of yore:–

Attend! for lo! amidst the din of waves,
  That on thy coast in thund'ring concert roll:–
Amidst each awful charm that Genius craves,
  At once to startle and to soothe the soul,

A minstrel's strain is heard! His trembling wire
  Attracts thy sons – once fam'd for war and song;
And, as thy scenes his varied verse inspire,
  Pleas'd Echo wakes, the numbers to prolong.

And well I ween such prospects might engage
  A loftier lay, did those who boast the flame
Of Heav'n-born Poesy, direct the age
  To find its pleasures in Britannia's fame.

........................................................

Yet thou, Cornubia, wilt not disregard
  A wight who fain would make thy merits known;
Not slight of the labours of a humble bard
  That weaves his votive verse to thee alone.

........................................................

Thou, like a miser, jealous of thy store,
  Conceal'st it from external gaze with care;

But who thy subterranean paths explore,
  In ev'ry varied form shall meet it there.

Metals, in nice graduation finely rang'd;
  Earths, of each diff'rent hue that artists know;
Primordial rocks, by time and chance unchang'd,
  Lie treasur'd 'midst thy wealthy hoards below.

And there – like Genius pining in the shade –
  Pure crystals oft dart forth the ardent ray
That show their worth; and when to light convey'd
  Give a new lustre to the glare of day.

.................................................................

These blended charms my willing muse would sing;
  And, in descriptive numbers, fain portray
What well might suit a more exalted string; –
  What yet may waken many a lofty lay.

Though hard the task, in measur'd strains to dress
  Pictorial objects; and their varied hues
And changeful features rightly to express,
  In colours such as Truth and Fancy chuse.

Yet haply, Application's patient toil
  O'er obstacles immense shall win her course;
And to Imagination paint the soil
  In sketches pregnant with poetic force.

And lo! a lovely prospect courts the eye!
  Behold where Tamer trails his length along!
Tamer! whose charms with prouder streams may vie,
  With thee the Muse begins her devious song.


# Roche Rock[3] and Hermitage

  Nigh where majestic Hensb'rough stands, –
The pride of Cornish mounds;
  From which th' astonish'd eye commands
A scene that scarce knows bounds:–

  Uprising from a barren heath, –
Abrupt, and vast, and high;

Roche Rock surveys the ground beneath
With cold, unkindred eye.

Amidst a wild and moss-clad waste
His granite brow ascends;
And o'er the plain, by flow'r ungraced,
A length'ning shadow lends.

And Science long shall wond'ring seek
How, – bare to ev'ry storm –
On earth as unallied as bleak,
Arose its stranger-form.

Projecting o'er the rock's rough side,
With plain, yet graceful brow;
An ancient tow'r, in lonely pride,
Nods to the waste below.

Besieg'd by elemental wars, –
To ev'ry blast a prey,
The fabric shews the num'rous scars
Of Time and slow decay.

Its roof, its casements, and its doors,
Have yielded to the storm; –
Wild as the wide-surrounding moors,
It stands, a ruin'd form.

The rank grass wavers o'er its walls;
Its base is fill'd with weeds;–
Yet there no loathsome vermin crawls,
No pois'nous reptile breeds.

'Tis silent all, and lone as death,
Save when the rising gale
Indignant howls, with hollow breath,
And dares the pile assail.

Yet still enough remains to tell
What name the building bore; –
Beneath, a hermit's lonely cell, –
A mould'ring chapel o'er.

Still, peering through its eastern side
The arching window's seen; –
Beneath the op'ning that supplied
A feeble ray within.

And here, of old, – the world shut out –
A holy man retir'd,
  And, by austerities devout,
A sainted fame acquired.

  Seldom he left his lonely cell
To pace the neighb'ring wild;
  Content, in solitude to dwell, –
To mis'ry reconcil'd.

  Yet oft, at midnight's solemn hour,
When Nature lay asleep;
  He climb'd his isolated tow'r
To watch, and pray, and weep;

  And deem'd the world and all its toys
Well lost, so he might find,
  'Midst Contemplation's sober joys,
The sunshine of the mind.


# Botallack[4]

  Contagious here, Botallack's wealthy mine,
By enterprise distinguish'd, – whose design
Cold Prudence had survey'd with fear and pain –
Rewards th' advent'rous band with lib'ral gain.
While young the undertaking's infant state,
And none could dare predict its future fate,
To prosecute the works so newly made
Immense machin'ry must afford its aid.
Down the steep precipice whose giddy height
Might fill the stoutest mortal with affright,
By cranking crane, and squeaking pullies slung,
The vast steam-engine o'er the rude cliffs rung!
Fearless and free from harm, the daring crew,
Help'd by its pow'r, their steady course pursue;
Through sullen rocks they bore their arduous way
And on the solid masses ope the day.
Nor here their course they check'd: Beneath the wave
That far above their heads was heard to rave; –
Beneath the deep Atlantic's spacious bed,
On either side their cavern'd paths are spread?
The filt'ring drops that ooze, successive, through,
Excite their zeal, more closely to pursue

The metallif'rous vein, ere chance or change
Forbid their vent'rous footsteps thus to range
The submarine abyss; and turn their toil,
Reluctant, to a less endanger'd soil.

**Henry Quick 1792–1857**

# The Life and Progress of Henry Quick of Zennor

*Part One*

My Christian friends, both far and near,
Both high and low, pray lend an ear,
While I my birth and life reveal,
I trust your hearts will for me feel.

Henry is my Christian name,
And Quick of course by nature came:
Old England is my native plain,
God did create and me sustain.

'Twas on fair Cornwall's north-west shore,
On Zennor's coast, December four,
Seventeen hundred ninety-two,
Born was I in this world of woe.

My parents they were honest poor,
Just kept the wolf from off the door;
My father laboured underground,
Mother the spinning-wheel put round.

When I was but a little child,
Convulsion-fits soon drove me wild,
As teeth were cutting in my head
I many minutes lay as dead.

Which surely gave me violent pain,
Affected much my head and brain;
My eyeballs did distressed roll,
Whilst many laugh'd and thought me fool.

Nor did I seem to note or know,
As other children mostly do;
For I was in a sad strange way,
My tender parents oft did say.

My mother of me took great care,
Me hardly out of sight could bear,
Whilst other little boys were free
To play, I wanted liberty.

When I was in my six years old,
A sad adventure I'll unfold,
Happened to me one Summer's day,
As I with mother took my way.

'Twas through a croft, by the wayside,
An adder in the ditch I spied;
The thing did look so fine and gay,
I felt inclin'd with it to play.

Quite ignorant and innocent,
What by its speckl'd back was meant,
I instantly my hand put down,
To take it up from off the ground.

The moment I had done this thing,
It sprang and stuck and pierc'd its sting,
Which was so sharp and poisonous strong,
Into the palm, and fast it hung.

My mother dear was sore affright,
When she look'd back and saw the sight,
It caus'd her to lament and cry,
And said that I should surely die.

No, mother, if I die don't cry,
I unto her did then reply;
She straightway took me by the hand,
And to a neighbour's house she ran.

Where she did show the dismal wound,
If any cure could there be found;
In tears she earnestly did cry,
Their skill to try, lest I should die.

The poison had begun to fly,
My hand, head, face swell'd dreadfully;
An old man took a razor keen,
The wounded place cut through the skin.

Blood, black as soot, did then appear,
Then came the same both fresh and clear;
Then milk and rinds of ash they found,
And wash'd, and rubb'd, and dress'd my wound.

The swelling then did soon abate,
And then my parents' joy was great;

A surgeon next the same did view,
Who said they'd done what's right and true.

Then physic next for me was brought,
Which soon a perfect cure wrought;
A purple mark doth always stand,
Upon the back of my right hand.

When I was eight years old, indeed,
Mother put me to school to read;
Though slow at first I seem'd to take,
Yet soon I did a progress make.

Of what I read, the greatest part,
I very soon had got by heart;
Borrow'd much books and read them through
And bought a quantity also.

Many good people of each degree,
Sev'ral fine books did give to me,
And in the same I took delight,
My constant study day and night.

Yet one sad thing I must reveal,
When I had read them over well,
The leaves I tore asunder, they
Delighted me with them to play.

My father angry grew apace,
He burned them before my face,
Severely then corrected me,
The folly of such tricks to see.

Soon after that I did reclaim,
And much repented of the same;
As careless then of books I'd been,
So careful now of them I'm seen.

Chapters and stories could repeat,
With every syllable complete;
I likewise learn'd in little time
To write, and then composed rhyme.

*Part Two*

When I was in my thirteenth year,
I lost my tender father dear,

Consumption brought him down to death,
And stopp'd his last vital breath.

Just at the age of fifty-one,
His glass was run, his life was gone;
I trust the Saviour, all in all,
Took pity on his precious soul.

'Twas in eighteen hundred and five,
April the eighth, he ceased to live;
In T'wednack churchyard there doth lie,
His dust to rest till the last day.

A favourite horse, call'd Punch by name,
My father sold the very same,
While he was laid on his death-bed,
Ere his immortal spirit fled.

Poor mother then was left with me,
In this wide world of misery,
To toil and struggle up and down,
Should fortune smile, or fate should frown.

But the all-wise, forever blest,
Father and friend of the distrest,
He by his providential care,
Protected me and mother dear.

Glory be to his holy name,
He was, now is, and ever the same;
Mysterious are his works and ways,
All things shall turn unto his praise.

When father died I had not learn'd
One single penny then to earn;
My mother by her toil and pain,
Had me thus wholly to maintain.

My father, he, at Lady Downs,
Leased a few acres of croft ground,
And built a little cottage there,
High rent thirty shillings per year.

Of which he small improvement made,
Before he in the grave was laid;
So poor and barren it became,
Mother resolved to sell the same.

When two long years had rolled round,
She sold the same for twenty pounds;
A cottage, thirty shilling rent,
Five years we liv'd in, till 'twas spent.

We then grew poorer every day,
Were forced to beg some parish pay;
From door to door went up and down,
From street to street, from town to town.

Please to bestow your charity
On a poor boy distress'd like me;
Affected are my head and brain
By fits, I oft-times did complain.

Some would take pity and relieve
Victuals and pence unto me give;
But some again would nought but frown,
Through envy strive to pull me down.

But bless the Lord, who kind has been,
And led me by a hand unseen;
O may I praise his holy name,
And give him glory for the same.

I did to riper years arrive,
And then some other means contrive,
To earn my bread by industry,
And not depend on charity.

When in my twenty-seventh year,
Measles did then on me appear;
When I was aged thirty-one,
Small-pox my body over-run.

My stature is five feet ten,
Though not the handsomest of men:
The great all-wise who formed me,
As his good pleasure so I be.

We gather'd brooms and got them bound,
And sold them to the country round;
Who wants a broom? Be pleased to buy,
I've got good ones, can you supply.

This calling though 'twas honesty,
Yet evil ones would frown on me,

Threaten and order me away,
I should not steal the heath they'd say.

Sometimes a little job I found,
To dig potatoes or break ground;
Cutting of turf and peat also,
A little I did sometimes do.

At last some good gentleman,
Took pity and did me befriend;
Commended much my poetry,
And got them printed off for me.

My printed copies then did sell,
And people seem'd to like them well;
Parish to parish, town to town,
I travell'd through and sold them round.

In selling books I took delight,
Oft-times abroad to take my flight,
And store my mind with subjects new,
But let them be what's just and true.

Be pleas'd to buy my little book,
And don't despise nor overlook;
Please to take pity on poor Henny,
I love to gain an honest penny.

And may the Lord my mind dispose,
On worthy subjects to compose,
That they may good examples be,
And useful to posterity.

O Lord, on me, thy grace bestow,
To learn and keep thy holy law;
Sweet Saviour cleanse my soul from sin,
Renew my heart and mind within.

Forgive my sins and follies past,
And grant me grace while life shall last;
The remnant of my mortal days
Let me devote unto thy praise.

Let not thy blood be shed in vain,
Dear Lord, let me be born again;
Like Happy Dick live humble I,
And like poor Joseph may I die.

O let me learn to be content,
And not repine at what is sent;
In want or plenty, health and pain,
Like Job may patience me sustain.

Like patient Job may I be blest,
And count all things still for the best;
Let me have lively faith in God,
All things together work for good.

O let me have some good employ,
My meat and drink thus to enjoy,
However mean soe'er it be,
O let me live by honesty.

And unity and peace and love,
That heaven may bless me from above;
Lord, give me faith to call on thee,
And from all evil set me free.

God's Sabbaths let me ne'er despise,
But read good books, learnt to be wise,
Go to his house, and hear his word,
Sing hymns, and pray, and seek the Lord.

A country life will suit me best,
A city life's no peace nor rest;
Such life will never do for me,
A country peasant let me be.

On good potatoes oft I share,
And barley bread my homely fare;
Pottage and milk, most wholesome food;
Bless God these things are very good.

Though some may slight and me disdain
Should I of poverty complain;
The Lord can succour my distress,
He will not leave me comfortless.

Though some may laugh and at me game
Nought else but fools would do the same;
No laughing matter to despise,
The mighty works of the all-wise.

Mocking is catching, it is said,
Such thoughts should fill the mind with dread;

They are not mocking at the creature,
They're only mocking their Creator.

What sad examples have been shown,
On many who were mockers known;
Some wounded sore, or stricken dead,
Or strengthless seized, or senses fled.

Lord, banish malice from my mind,
To pride nor passion be inclin'd.
Let me in love and meekness live,
Learn to forget and to forgive.

My mortal age now fifty-one,
Of fleeting years are past and gone;
Let me my precious time redeem,
In matters of the most esteem.

Now while as yet 'tis call'd today,
How swift my time does pass away;
I ne'er can call it back again,
Lord let it not be spent in vain.

*Part Three*

Now dearest friends, I next proceed,
Briefly for to relate with speed,
My mother's death, my marriage too,
And heavy trials I went through.

Twenty-nine years were past and gone,
Since my poor father's glass was run,
Eleven weeks likewise past by,
My poor old mother then did die.

The last seven years she did exist,
A cancer grew within her breast
No surgeon's skill could her befriend,
This fatal wound her life did end.

Monday the twenty-third of June,
That morn her mortal glass was run,
In eighteen hundred thirty-four;
I trust she's safe on Canaan's shore.

Seventy-five years, and three months space,
Were on this earth her mortal race,

The latter years she did remain,
Were spent in sorrow, grief and pain.

Her soul by death is called home,
Her flesh consigned to the tomb,
In Zennor churchyard underground,
To rest till the last trump shall sound.

Then when the Lord comes in the air,
O may we meet together there;
O that will be a joyful day,
All death, pain, parting done away.

Poor mother being dead and gone,
I in distress was left alone;
But the almighty did me guide,
And still he doth for me provide.

A good and tender mother she,
No earthly friend so kind to me;
My company by night and day,
My head, and chief support, and stay.

A little country cot did rent,
And struggled on with sweet content;
Many-a-one prov'd friendly kind,
And good to me, which cheer'd my mind.

But now came on sharp trials strong,
Some secret foes did me great wrong,
Their lying tongues soon spread around,
That I'd got sav'd many a pound.

God witness be, I truth confess,
One single pound I didn't possess,
Should death this day my portion be,
I've not enough to bury me.

I've found since mother's dead and gone,
One trouble did not come alone;
My near relations, verily,
My greatest foes have proved to be.

They all forsook me in distress,
And left my mind quite comfortless;
Was any thing that they could gain
From me, they would have spar'd no pain.

Some secret foes commended me,
Unto a loose and faithless she;
To whom I was by marriage vows,
To be the tender loving spouse.

Although our banns in church were call'd,
The same for good was overrul'd;
I suffered full ten shillings loss,
Which was to me a bitter cross.

When she did view my humble home,
And found that riches I had none,
She quickly turn'd her back on me,
And never more my face would see.

But God, I trust, this trial blest,
And made all things work for the best;
Had she become my wedded wife,
It might have cost my precious life.

O may I never be dismayed,
Trust in the Lord, be not afraid,
To be my providential friend,
Whose love and mercy knows no end.

He did support me all my days,
To his great name be all the praise,
And sent many good friends to me,
When oft-times in extremity.

Bless God my health is very good,
I still enjoy my homely food;
O may I thank him for the same,
And bless and praise his holy name.

At forty-three I took a wife,
To be my guide through future life;
For I was very much distress'd.
Quite desolate and comfortless.

October the twenty-fifth day,
Eight fleeting years have pass'd away,
Since eighteen hundred thirty-five,
I entered into marriage life.

My poor wife, she was born and bred,
By constant toil to get her bread;

Her mortal age, it now appears,
Is just three score and fifteen years.

Although her strength is almost spent,
Her mind is still on labour bent;
But by the means of cruel foes,
I have experienced many woes.

Uncivil treatment, most unkind,
Has much destroyed my peace of mind,
By means of strife and discontent,
Through blame of what I'm innocent.

Cursed are those who maketh strife,
And discord cause 'twixt man and wife;
And such as easy do believe,
A lying tongue will soon deceive.

Yet though by cruel foes belied,
And my poor mind severely tried,
The Lord above all things doth know,
I trust his grace will bring me through.

Eight tedious years of grief and strife,
I've suffer'd with a jealous wife,
Her discontent torments me sore,
Suspicious I have paltry store.

Display thy power, O God of might,
My wrongs discover, and bring to light,
By some wise means, through life or death,
Before that I resign my breath.

Poverty is a grievous trouble,
But harsh reflection makes it double,
When poverty in doors doth hie,
Out window love doth swiftly fly.

Content and peace is all I crave,
Nor noise or strike I wish to have;
My all-wise maker, ever blest,
Doth order all things for the best.

Though poor and mean should be my lot,
Let sweet content dwell in my cot;
Disdain no humble life to live,
With gratitude ask and receive.

Now to conclude what I have penn'd,
I trust the Lord will stand my friend,
And give me grace while here on earth,
And endless glory after death.

**H**as **E**nvy **N**ever **R**eigned? **Y**es:
**Q**uite **U**nlike **I**s **C**hristian **K**indness.[1]
Observe the same, remember me,
For here my name you plainly see.

# The Death of Pascoe Semmens, 1826

Dear mortal friends and neighbours lend an ear,
A shocking accident I now declare;
How soon we're smitten by the darts of death,
How suddenly the Lord may stop our breath.

Poor Pascoe Semmens as for truth I tell,
Of Ludgvan Parish as 'tis known full well;
By lightning blasted, turn'd to silent clay,
And on the ground a breathless corpse did lay.

This awful shock on Friday afternoon,
Took place near four o'clock the ninth of June;
A heavy thunder storm from east did rise,
Dark foggy clouds did gather through the skies.

The morning fine and pleasant did appear,
The weather hot, the sun shone bright and clear;
For six weeks space there scarce fell any rain,
For want of showers many did complain.

Poor Pascoe Semmens that morning as we hear,
With cart and horses cheerful did repair;
From Trazza village he sets off with speed,
To Castle Dennis Downs he did proceed.

His father-in-law's own turves that very day,
To carry home intended was they say;
His brother-in-law John Hosking a grown lad,
Was mostly with him pitchman as 'tis said.

The morning passed on as we do hear,
At noon he home to dinner did repair;
And after dinner thus to be refesh'd,
For a short time compos'd himself to rest.

It was not long sweet slumber clos'd his eyes,
He suddenly was called to arise;
Some heavy showers threaten to descend,
'Tis best with speed our present work to end.

He started up just half awake 'tis said,
To downs then with all haste that could be made;
Dismal and gloomy did the sky appear,
And distant thunders were approaching near.

Having arriv'd and nearly made an end,
The threatening storm then downwards did descend;
Fierce lightning flashed, heavy showers did fall,
Loud claps of thunder roll'd from pole to pole.

He said to his young comrade, "Make haste drive on,
Dispatch with speed and let us home begone;
I'm wet to skin for every drop comes through,
More good those showers have done than we can do."

Just as he spoke those words and made an end,
A heavy shower of hail there did descend;
A dreadful thunder clap succeeds the same,
A blaze of lightning broke forth in a flame.

Poor Pascoe smote, fell lifeless to the ground,
By lightning struck received death's mortal wound;
One of the horses likewise kill'd stone dead,
The other also stun'd some time was laid.

His young comrade stood as we understand,
Four feet distance pitching some few brands;
Felt an uncommon stroke which knock'd him down,
Senseless some time he lay upon the ground.

He says as he was falling to the ground,
He saw both horses likewise smitten down;
Like one awake from sleep he lifts his eyes,
But finds himself unable to arise.

Poor Pascoe's naked body he espies,
Behind the cart-wain, as he cast his eyes;
At four feet distance from the cart he found,
Fallen on his back extended on the ground.

He tries but could not speak, when him he sees,
He then crawls forth upon his hands and knees;

Finds him a breathless corpse, was frighted sore,
His dear companion Pascoe was no more.

He left him there and straightaway home did go,
And gave his friends the dreadful news to know;
They all mistrusted when they saw his face,
Some awful accident had taken place.

Poor Pascoe's corpse was home with speed convey'd,
On Sunday afternoon in dust was laid;
Coroner and Jury gave their verdict good,
"By visitation of Almighty God."

He aged was but twenty-nine last May,
He married was about three years they say;
A loving husband peaceable and mild,
A loving wife and only one sweet child.

He left his loving wife in tears to mourn,
Her dearest husband that will ne'er return;
"Little did I think," says she, "when out of door,
He took his leave to speak to me no more."

He useful learning from a child was taught,
To read and write most excellent was brought;
Cheerful and sober was as we do hear,
And duly did frequent the house of prayer.

Above two thousand persons there did come,
To see him laid within the silent tomb;
His loving friends did mourn for him full sore,
Alas! he's gone, poor Pascoe is no more.

His withered body in the dust must lay,
Until the last great resurrection day;
The trump shall sound, ten thousand thunders roar,
Shall cleave the ground and all the dead restore.

Loud calls around us from the Lord are sent,
And yet rebellious sinners won't repent;
God's awful judgement's through the earth abroad,
"Sinners awake! Prepare to meet your God!"

O sinner should the Lord in vengeance frown
Where wilt thou run if justice cuts thee down?
Thy soul would drop into a burning hell,
Where none but damned souls and devils dwell.

Repent with speed and rightly be advis'd,
Before another thunder storm should rise;
If thus prepar'd no need hast thou to fear,
Though stricken dead shalt swift to heaven repair.

Now to conclude these lines and make an end,
Of these most awful verses I have penn'ed;
Prepare, Awake, Seek Christ, Obey, Endure,
Strive, Every, Means Make Election Now Sure.[2]

## Acrostic on John Verrant of St Hilary, 1835

Jesus thou bleeding lamb of God,
O wash me in thy cleansing blood,
Have mercy on my soul I pray,
Now lead me in the living way.
Virtue and inward holiness
Eternal God let me possess,
Ruin'd and lost by Adam's fall,
Restore me Saviour All in All,
A free and full redemption give.
Now guide me while on earth I live,
Then after death to Heaven receive.

## The Death of John Martyns, 1836[3]

Mortals high and low, attention
Give to what I shall relate;
A most solemn scene I mention,
A poor young man's sudden fate.

Leaving his dear home one morning,
In the midst of life and prime,
Soon was locked in the bowels
Of the earth sent out of time.

Such untimely fate attended
Poor John Martyn called by name,
As he underground descended
And was crushed in the same.

This young man was bred a miner,
And did labour underground,

Where poor men ten thousand dangers
Constantly do them surround.

Born he was of honest parents,
And he was always much inclined
To be of a meek behaviour,
Patient and contented mind.

His poor mother is a widow,
His poor father some time dead,
Ludgvan was his native parish,
Where he was born and bred.

He was aged six and twenty,
Just about to take a wife,
In true love to be united,
And get settled through life.

Stout and tall in limbs and stature,
Strong and active, brisk and gay,
Full of life and health and vigour;
Soon a lump of lifeless clay.

'Twas December three and twentieth,
Friday morning just at ten,
Eighteen hundred six and thirty,
Did take place this solemn scene.

In the bowels of Wheal Tin Croft,
An old mine renew'd of late,
This poor young man he was labouring,
Where he met his sudden fate.

Down a shaft about ten fathoms,
Underground he did descend,
By the order of the captain;
Little thought his days to end.

A young lad descended with him,
William Curnow call'd by name,
Seven fathoms through a level,
Straight into a bolt they came.

Which was only eighteen inches
Square, about nine fathoms long,
On their hands and knees they creeped,
Only just could crawl along.

Then about a dozen fathoms
More, they through the adit came,
With a chain that they took with them,
Did take measure of the same.

They for sinking from the surface,
Through the level did intend,
A new shaft to the old bottom
Which stood at the level's end.

About forty years a standing
Choaked with water, mud and clay,
Which on their return from landing,
On poor Martyns broke away.

As 'twas known there was great danger,
He was charged to take great care,
Not a stone to move or meddle;
Yet he seemed void of fear.

As he struck some stones asunder,
Down the water, mud and clay
Soon did flow and filled the level,
With such force it broke away.

His comrade was got before him,
Through the bolt he just had passed,
When poor Martyns to him called,
"My both legs they are stuck fast.

Are you clear? I'm overtaken;
Let me on your legs lay hold;
Pull me out, I'm almost drowned,
Almost dead with wet and cold."

Curnow tried, but could not move him,
Though he strove with might and main;
Nine men tried their skill to clear him,
But alas, 'twas all in vain.

When they'd used their best endeavours,
And for him could do no more,
After all their toil and labour
They were forced to give him o'er.

Finding all means to deliver
Vain, poor Martyns he did say:

"'Tis no used to strive, I never
More shall see another day.

Loose the ropes and take them off me,
Leave me where I am to die;"
Then upon the Lord for mercy,
He most earnestly did cry.

Farewell dear friends and relations,
Mother, brothers, sisters dear,
Farewell now to my dear Sally,
Farewell to all worldly care.

Brother could embrace a brother,
How affecting 'twas to see,
And conversed with each other;
Yet they could not set him free.

Fondly thus they strove to cheer him,
But 'twas vain for anyone,
Meat or drink then to bring near him,
For his appetite was gone.

When his life was just departing,
And was giving up the ghost,
His dear brother went in to him,
And he found his speech was lost.

"Brother, can't you now speak to me?"
He did cry and sadly grieve;
But, alas, he could no answer,
From his dying lips receive.

Near four hours space it seemed,
He his vital breath retained,
Death his spirit then released,
Though his body still remained.

Twelve days in deep mud and water,
Close confined underground,
Till they'd sunk a pit eight fathoms,
To the place where he was drown'd.

One o'clock on Wednesday morning,
And the fourth of the New Year,
Was poor Martyn's lifeless body
Loosed and taken out the mire.

Home to his dear habitation,
They his body did convey,
And his funeral procession
Was the following Sabbath Day.

To Ludgvan Churchyard was carried,
His poor lifeless lump of clay,
In his silent dust interred
Till the Resurrection Day.

'Twas reported near six thousand
Did attend him to his tomb,
Who in the funeral rites most solemn
Guarded him to his long home.

His dear soul we trust is landed,
Safely on the Heavenly Shore,
Where all greed and sorrow's ended,
Pain and parting are no more.

Now to make a full conclusion
Of these verses I have penned,
Lord make this our resolution,
To think on our latter end.


# John Uren of Boscrowan, 1847

Our aged brother Uren is dead,
His soul has took its flight
To dwell with Christ his heavenly head,
We trust in realms of light.

A native he of Gulval was,
Born was on Christmas Day,
The day our blessed Saviour thus
Was born on earth they say.

In seventeen hundred seventieth year
After that blessed event,
Our aged friend as doth appear
Into this world was sent.

In early days from his youth up
He trod the worldly way,
Inclined to take a little drop,
Was merry light and gay.

Estranged was his heart from God,
And from his holy ways,
His holy names did reverence not,
Nor lived to his praise.

When he was nearly fifty years
Of age, he did begin
For to discern, as it appears,
The wretchedness of sin.

One night he had a horrid dream
As on his bed he lay,
Satan appeared unto him
His soul to take away.

With him he fought a desperate fight,
And could not from him flee,
Which waked him in great affright,
But Christ did set him free.

He joined the people of the Lord,
And learned to watch and pray;
His sacred church and holy word
Each blessed Sabbath day.

Duly attended and did read,
And strove with all his might,
By steadfast faith in Christ to seek
A city out of sight.

From all intoxicating drink
For twenty-seven years
He did abstain, and serious think
With true repentant tears.

Nearly nine years as doth appear
A widower was he,
Eleven children he did rear
By care and industry.

Four now are dead, seven still survive,
Four of them married are,
In mortal life to toil and strive
By providential care.

The little farms he did possess,
His property and store,

Unto his children he has left,
On earth he'll be no more.

The last six months he did sojourn
Below ere life expired,
He gave up family concern
And went to live retired.

About six weeks before his death
He did converse with me,
'Twas the last time his face on earth
I evermore did see.

He said above sixty years past,
He did remember well
John Wesley preach at Gear, how Christ
The lunatic did heal.

Short illness closed his mortal days,
Death soon did lay him down,
Though constitution was always
Through life both firm and sound.

Upon the eighteenth day of March
In eighteen forty seven,
His soul did from this world depart,
We trust to enter heaven.

The day before he did depart
This life, he did reply,
My work is done, Christ in my heart,
I'm not afraid to die.

Fifteen weeks fleeting space ran on,
Since our dear friend consigned
Was to the dust, when James his son
His vital breath resigned.

By short and fatal fierce disease,
Leaving in tears to mourn
Six children and a pregnant wife,
Where he'll no more return.

We trust the Lord of life and death,
Who rules both earth and sky,
Hath took their spirits from this earth
To dwell with him on high.

# William Thomas of Boswednack

William Thomas, of Boswednack,
Father of twenty-three under wedlock.
All his family he did rear,
By industry, toil and care.
He has gained the highest prize
Of twenty-four parishes.
He is an example rare
Of diligence and godly fear.
May God bless him and his race,
Thus to spend their days in grace;
May their latter end be peace,
Heavenly joys that never cease.

# Our Cornish Drolls Are Dead

Our Cornish drolls are dead, each one;
The fairies from their haunts have gone;
There's scare a witch in all the land,
The world has grown so learn'd and grand.

**John Tabois Tregellas 1792–1863**

## *From* St Agnes Bear Hunt

"We caan't stand this, ef we be men,
　　To see our cheldurn deer
Toar lemb from lemb, and their heart's blood
　　Sucked by a furrin' Beer.

Aw! lev us rise, – Aw! lev us rise,
　　My nibours lev us rise,
We'll kill the monster ef we can,
　　Or teer out boath hes eyes.

Lev ev'ry man that es a man
　　And ev'ry boy that es
As laarge as little men, git armed,
　　'Tes murder as it es.

We'll arm ourselves with ugly things,
　　Stoanes, biddixes,[1] and boords,
And picks and gads,[2] and showls and dags,[3]
　　And bagonetts and swoords.

Then lev us go in millyons down
　　To Dirtypool, – and mind,
Up to Wheal Kitty arterwards,
　　Where thousands we shall find."

So off to Dirtypool the throng
　　Of *Cousin Jackies*[4] went,
Up to Wheal Kitty, where they stopped
　　As if by one consent.

Then Captain Peard so eloquent
　　A fresh speech did commence,
Remarkable for energy
　　And its uncommon sense.

"Lev all your hinguns[5] idle stand,
　　Lev noane to work be found,
Doan't lev a kibble[6] down a shaft,
　　No lev a whem[7] go round.

Boath tutwork men[8] and tributers,[9]
　　And halvaners,[10] I say,
Lev every man that es a man
　　Come forth weth me to-day.

Be quick and turn up every reck,
    Lev all your buddles[11] go,
Your trunks[12] and covers[13] never mind,
    To-day it must be so.

Your cobbin' hammers[14] weth ee bring,
    Caal up the deffurnt coors,[15]
And every stem-man[16] lev un come,
    And they upon the floors."

Now when the marshalled host so strong,
    To Goonlaze Downs did reach,
Peard, like a valiant General, made
    Another warlike speech.

"All you what knawed what sodgering was
    When you belonged unto
The great say fencibles, shaw now
    What Cornish blood can do."

## *From* Rozzy Paul and Zacky Martin

At Towan Porth (that's what they call
The place) was born one Rozzy Paul,
And there, likewise, did live "for sartin,"
Another miner, Zacky Martin.
But westward wandered these queer souls
And laboured in "St Ives Consols."
Each rented in the town, tho' poor,
A house which boasted a "fore door,"
By which they rose to men of note,
And were entitled to a vote, −
Potwollopers their appellation,
Who pocket bribes to sell the nation.
    One day, a long, long while ago,
The date I don't profess to know,
Or whether such was right or wrong,
(Enough for me to write my song,
And tell you of Saint Ives Election,
With all its fun and imperfection).
The town was all "alive and kicking,"
And friends were friends to pieces picking;
Drinking, bribing, swearing, lying,
Flags and scandal thickly flying,
Some of the mottoes, history states,
Were "Fish and Plenty," "Hakes and Tates,"

"No scads nor Rays," "No Staring Pies,"
"Starling for ever! he's prize."
      But who stands there with hat in hand.
With gracious smiles and looks so bland.
The other party at him snarling?
Silence! – a speech, – Sir Walter Starling.
      "Men of St Ives!" – he began,
"In me you see an honest man,
To do you good is my design,
*Your* interests ever shall be *mine*;
And soon I hope, my friends, to see
You independent, rich, and free:
I'm well convinced it's a mistake
About your 'whipping of the hake,'
And when in Parliament I sit,
For which, it seems, you think me fit,
For Pilchards I'll new markets find,
With prices sure to please your mind;
Instead of Congers, Rays and Hakes,
Roast beef shall smoke upon your plates;
The best of cheer shall be your lot,
And for your wives, silk gowns I've brought."
      Says Zack to Rozzy, "That's clain off,
The tother man es but a snoff;
Sir Walter Starling es our man,
We'll do for he now all we can."
      With groans from some, from others cheers,
The famed Sir Bullion Bragg appears,
Full of fine promises and chaff
And ready in his sleeve to laugh;
He waved his hand, and smiled and bowed,
And thus addressed the noisy crowd: –
"Electors of St Ives, behold!
I'll make your streets o'erflow with gold;
The Indian fleet shall here resort,
Be manned and victualled at this port;
When in the *House* my seat is filled,
I'll introduce an act to build
A breakwater of marvellous strength,
A mile or two, or more, in length;
I'll treble too the pilchard bounty
Paid by the Treasury to this County;
And women whom I love most dearly
Shall all be votes, – I speak sincerely;
I'll build for Hakes, you'll have such trade in 'em,
A factory for marinading 'em;
I'll find you sales in Egypt, – there O!
In Alexandra and Grand Cairo,

There smoking Mussulmans shall watch 'em,
And eat them faster than you catch 'em;
The ladies of St Ives shall get,
(The climate here being rather wet),
Either to use them or to swing 'em,
Rich silk umbrellas, – mind, nor gingham."
    This startling eloquence of Bragg's
Beat poor Sir Walter's all to rags;
His oily words and bribes so pleasant,
Gained his election for the present.
    "Bribing," says Zacky, "es a sin,
And Bullion tried to take me in;
I seed un give a man five pound,
Thoft I, 'twill be the saame all 'round;
But offered me, now doan't ee see,
Instead of five pound awnly three."
    "These words," said Rozzy, "too, I heerd,
To swear 'tes so I baant affeerd;
I waant chait Maaster Starling, nor
Be chaited nuther, – no, – what for?
That this es brib'ry, (who can doubt it;
We'll tell Sir Watty's lawyer 'bout it.")
The lawyer soon made out the case,
And a petition next took place;
Bullion's election must be undone,
And Zack and Roz must go to London.

.........................................................

At once our heroes fell to work,
And well they plied the knife and fork;
However thick was cut each slice,
Their plates were emptied in a trice.
Now Rozzy made a sudden stop,
And said, "Sir Waalter, will ee swop,
I've got the fat and you the lain, –
Swop waun for t'other's what I main."
This was as quickly done as said,
The rude exchange he quickly made;
The lean which he so strongly wished,
Out of Sir Walter's plate he fished,
And with the fork that took the piece,
Returned *his* plate's superfluous grease.
Many such strange things did occur,
Nor dared Sir Walter once demur,
For as they came his cause to favour,
He could but wink at their behaviour,
And only laughed, while they laughed more,
And kept the table in a roar.

To finish off, Zack ate a pine,
And drank at least three pints of wine;
And then it was arranged that they
(Our Cornishmen) the following day
Should to the House of Commons go,
And strike the great decisive blow.
      So Rozzy and his comrade went
Like greater men to Parliament;
The adventures there which them befell,
I have not room or time to tell;
How in Committee Rooms they swore,
And made the gravest members roar;
How brazen barristers were vexed,
And lawyers with their words perplexed;
Suffice to say, they gained the case,
And bragging Bullion lost his place.

## William Sandys 1792–1874

# Visit to Lunnon

Dost thee knaw, Sos,[1] I've ben up to Lunnon[2] church-town?
A fine passel of things I seed theere to put down.
Were I sliced ento slivers so thin as a straw,
I cud na tell thee haalf the braave things as I saw.
Why, now, what do 'ee thenk? they've got timberen roadds,
Which es fitty at times, but for quilkins,[3] and toaads;
Pure sport for tom-toddies, or a padgitepooe:[4]
And when et do come, cheel, but a bit of a skew,
Why the rain et do make em so slippy, and slottery,
'Tes no wonder they hosses, do get stogged, or trot awry.
Then the Cabs as they caalls 'em, keeps pooten about,
Like an Angletich twisten etself en and out.
And they 'Busses of which then, plase sure, there's a mort,
Skeyse about like the bilers of ingines en sport.
Well cheel, as for the shops I were quite en a maaze,
'Fath I ne'er seed sich beauties en all my boorn daays.
There es some with out-wenders as laarge as the housen,
All prink'd oop so pridy, weth there picters, and cloase en.
And then, ef I ever! sich fine tummals[5] of cloam,
They make a scat marchant of they spaars up toe hoam.
For the maaids thee mays't see to such nackins and gownds,
And sich aperns and coats; I'd as lieve as two pounds,
That my wife bea'nt slocked in thickey notions to see,
For my fangings wud look scoy and wished ef so be.
She've jist caal'd me a cropeing timdoodle i' facks,
'Caase of cuyn I ded gev her less than she ded axe.
Then plase sure, there's no cause to be creening, or dreuling,
Be bedoled[6] weth the rheumatic, roadling, or puling.
For there's doctors as pomsters all sorts of diseases:
Thee art paltcht oop quite braave like whenever thee pleases.
What's the odds, if thee'rt scat all abroad? 'tes a pity,
But en few hours vallee, thee'rt flam new, and fitty.[7]
And then as to their saaves they's got sich a command on,
They clopping like corns, ha'nt a foot left to stand on.
Thee'st be sure that I went for to see they play-actors,
And they told I that they shaw'd some famousest caracturs.
I caan't tell 'ee the neame, but once there comed en
A fellor weth breeches and weth coat all of tin.
Then they caal'd him a goast, and they made wise to staart:
For a buch-a-boo[8] thof he did seem cruel smaart.
And a comrade en black weth the shivers were took,
And he squinnied, tell I were nigh shrimmed weth es look;
Thrawed es hat on the planchen, and ded kicky rayther,
Then next he comed out, "How do 'ee fadge royal feyther?

Why's thee en sich a takeing? things doesn't seem suant,"
Says the goast, "Ooncle Clodgy's ben playen the truant,
He gove me a scat en the chacks for the nonce,
Then wethout being caal'd out, he ded marry to once
Your mother; because why, I were perfectly dead,
And it were all along of that whap en the head.
But, I tell 'ee what, Sos, dont 'ee lev him alone."
"Why plase sure then I wain't," said es cheeld with a groan;
That's es comraade, 'twere Hamlet I mind were es naame,
And he tarvied about, and sed 'twere a big sheame.
Well then, down a great shaaft foes the man latteen,
As et were the man Ingine,[9] up to Tresavean.
Then Hamlet hisself did fetch about like one mazed;
Drove a maiden, weth whom he keeped company, crazed:
And sent she to Passion, for a nun ef so be,
'Caase he cudn't afford for to have none of she.
The young 'oman herself en a pond were found dead,
And the Crowner's 'quest vardict said, she were drownded.
At laast comed ould Ooncle, and a skrimmage and strow;
And they all thraw'd each other, so ended that show.
Then a passel of maidens comed en to the pleace,
Each so smaart thee caan't think, weth a pure roagish feace:
And beginn'd for to skeyce and to fade so friskis,
Why they seemed to my mind like a passel of piskeys,
But their coasts were so short – I'm asheamed – why I sees –
As – 'es I ded 'fath – auh! – quite up to the knees.
Sich a guakum were I, that I first turned my feace,
But were forced to turn back, to make sure 'twere the caase.
And then to be sure, 'twere a cruel fine shew;
Dont 'ee laught – 'tes the dauncing I means, thee do knaw.
'Fore the parlement mimbers the next day I goes,
To tell 'pon the rail-roaads, what so be I suppose.
From St Joost[10] to the Loggan's[11] one thee'st may depend,
Weth a braanch to Tol Pedn, and one to Laand's End.
What powers of folks sure, there comed in to gaape,
I were squabb'd 'gen the durnes, I were en a fine shaape;
Sich pocks and sich touzing, and when I had scrouged en, I
Seed the pleace jist about wern't so laarge as my linney.
Well, when I fetched en too, sich a scavel and gow
I ne'er heerd afore sure, why possed oop en a row
Was a score or some counsellors, all en discoose,
And a josing, and tearing, and making good coose.
About some'at they was so polrumptuous got,
Ef haalf sed two was two, t'other haalf sed 'twas not.
Well they argufied then, ef the roaad were but maade,
There wud be there for sarten, a pure stem of traade,
And began for to axe of my comraades and I,
To tell up all they things, we thoft wud be carr'd by.

All the cotches, the wains, and the butts, all the gaffers,
And all the gammers, the childer, the hosses, the yeffers;
And sich mashes of turmits, and tubbans, and turves,
Fish, poltaties, and straunger, (which laast they observes
Will en scools be like pilchers,) the scaal milk, and veers,
Moils, poldavy,[12] tin-stuff, copper ore, and mabyers,[13]
With carts, Bal-girls, and gooses, and appuls, and cows.
Why they ouft to count choughs too and padgetepows.
Then they thoft et a pity rail-roads was not maade,
Thof 'twere not for their fangings they cried up that traade.
Ef they tried for to slock us, 'twere all for the best,
And our fortins was maade, ef our cuyn we ded 'vest.
Now I warny that there might be all pure and fitty,
Ef so be I were to the purvisioned committee;
But then, doubting says I, thickey might be the caase,
'Tes well for to fetch hoam, and lev out from this plaace.
Then they some'at commerced about stags and stag-nation,
And that ef we was stagg'd 'twere for good of the naation.
But 'twud bust a long score of laayers, I tell 'ee,
To rise some of they rail-roaads, to fatch any vallee.

**Francis Hingeston 1796–1841**

## Sonnet Written at the Land's End

How sweetly solemn thy granite steep,
  Bolerium, 'mid the calm of earth and heaven,
To gaze upon the blue unbounded deep,
  What time with soften'd beam the orb or Even
Stoops as to kiss it sleeping, while in air
  The sea-bird sails, and through the level ray
  Beneath the gilded bark pursues her way
O'er buried realms, awful, yet lovely fair.
Such was the scene to some glad hearts ere while
  Their 'country's bourne' presented, when, to mock
Its feebler charms, unto that beacon-rock
Ianthe came: beside her living smile
Dread Nature's grace seem'd gracious then no more,
And softened hearts forgot the fame of yore.

**Charles Taylor Stephens 1797–1863**

## *From* The Chief of Barat-Anac[1]

One Tuesday in bright sunny June,
Just as Saint Ives town-clock struck noon,
With loud, but sullen sound,
The first of Zennor's Rural Postmen,
A humble son of good Saint Crispin,
Thus musing, took his round.

"As there's a way where there's a will,
I'll see the Quoit on Zennor Hill,
And, from its rocky breast
I'll drag its long-lost history out;
And I'll dispell the clouds of doubt,
Which now do on it rest.

And thus I'll pass a happy hour,
In gath'ring truths from Wisdom's bower,
And gems to deck her crown.
I'll wreathe the sunbeams, as they play
Upon Old Neptune's trackless way
And gild his emerald throne."

Thus musing, Postman left St Ives,
Its pretty bay and prettier wives,
His duties to fulfill:
Passed through Consols, that wealthy mine,
Just at the time when stamp-boys dine,
And take of fun, their fill.

By Halse's and through Leger's towns,
Post onward went, to Rocky Downs,
To where the four roads meet;
Then Postman took Towednack road;
The face of day bore not a cloud,
But smiles, serene and sweet.

He pass'd Cold Harbour's barren waste,
And by Towednack church did haste,
Quite sanguine of success;
Reach'd "Beagle Tubban" in a trice,
And asked Dame Quick for her advice,
With all becoming grace.

Dame called poor Post a thorough fool,
And bade him go to Jan Green's school,
Where he might learn enough.
About the Cairn and Quoit, she said,
A thought had ne'er come in her head:
She did not mind such stuff.

He left her, and away did speed,
Not thinking, that in very deed,
Mist would his way enshroud;
But, Oh! 'Tis painful to relate,
The Hill, as if with him fun elate,
Its head thrust in a cloud!

It wrapp'd its nether parts in a fog,
As dense as ever circled bog,
Of Tam O'Shanter's fame;
But, Postman thought the road he knew,
And said, "though foggy, I'll pursue
My journey all the same."

In this dense fog, Post lost his way:
Poor Postman! Lack! O Lack-a-day!
What will the news-birds do?
If they their letters cannot have,
Like furies they will stamp and rave,
And surely make thee rue.

On, on he trudg'd; we cannot guess
How far he went: a mystery this:
To guess he never dared.
The Hill seem'd quite a mystery,
As vast as is the history
Of Pluto, so much fear'd.

At length a village met his sight;
'Twas Amalveor, with porches white;
Thither he ran to crave
Directions how he might regain
The road he'd lost, and how obtain
The knowledge he would have.

Good Farmer Will was in his barn,
Stripp'd to his waist, and thrashing corn;
To Will Post told his case,

And begg'd he'd tell him all he knew
About the Quoit, and legends too
Connected with the place.

Will, with good-humour'd gravity,
Said, "friend, I'll counsel give to thee,"
And, gazing on his phiz,
Said, "if the Quoit to-night you'd find,
Then, keep your head right to the wind,
You'll soon reach where it is.

But, as to legends, my advice
Is, think three times ere you act twice,
Or you will rue the day.
Pray, do not into secrets pry;
For round the Quoit, the Piskies lie;
They'll carry you away.

If any power on Earth e'er should
Remove the Quoit, I know it would
Be brought safe back again.
The witches' ghosts would bring it here,
So none you see, would ever dare
Attempt a task so vain!"

The Postman thank'd him, and resolv'd
He ne'er would rest until he'd solv'd
What so absorb'd his thought;
And, labouring up the mountain-side,
Keeping his head to wind, he tried
To reach the envied spot.

But this, in such a choaking fog,
Was too much for the Hampshire Hog;
It was a trial great;
For soon, exhausted, down he sat,
And slouching, seiz'd his dripping hat,
And cast it to his feet.

Then, with his fingers Post did throw
His dripping ringlets from his brow:
His grizzly beard he press'd:
He next his fog-drench'd coat did smooth;
And after that, he tried to sooth
His throbbing heart to rest.

In vain he strove to grasp his thoughts,
For they were scamp'ring like wild goats,

Around the swelt'ring mount,
Until he cast his longing gaze
Upward, and invok'd the blaze
Of light's exhaustless fount.

Who was it then, that did him great;
For Lo! Post startled to his feet,
And cheerfully did sing.
Twas Memory, cloth'd in living light:
She came, to give unbounded sight,
And loosen Fancy's string.

Before her presence, fog and rain
Withdrew; and, Luna's shining train
Did stoop to grace the spot;
The Illustr'ous Nine, in song attir'd,
Appear'd and Postman's nature fired;
Then Post found what he'd sought.

Around the Quoit, the Muses stand,
Forming as beautiful a band
As painter ever drew;
And Clio, with uplifted hand,
Ruling the soul-enrapturing band,
In notes melodious, gave command, –
"Sing to this Quoit in view!"

All hail! to the Noble Quoit
That graces Zennor Hill.
All hail! to the hallow'd rock;
It still its home does fill.
All hail! to the stars which deck
The Quoit's great hall of state.
All hail! to the beasts that were
Around this great Quoit slain.
All hail! to the men who bled
Its empire to maintain.
All hail! to the priest that made
Its flinty breast his seat.
All hail! to the noble ones
That worshipp'd at his feet.
All hail! to the chief that lies
Entomb'd within this mount.

**John Abraham 1798–c.1870**

## The Barren Mountain

My muse selects a lofty theme,
  I sing the mountain high;
No land of life, but a sad scene
  Of stern sterility –

Where winter holds perennial sway,
  Where storm and tempest blow,
Where the bright ruler of the day
  Shines on eternal snow.

Stupendous pile! I thee survey
  With heaven-directed gaze;
The mightiest works of man display
  Their puny littleness.

Methinks when Nature gave thee birth,
  And bade thy summit rise
Above the prostrate things of earth,
  Majestic in the skies,

To check thy pride the Almighty Power,
  That decks the vale below,
Forbade a single vernal flower
  To adorn thy barren brow.

Fresh opening to the solar ray,
  The woodland beauties blow;
But changing seasons, green and gay,
  Thy regions never know.

No winged minstrel there shall dwell,
  Sweet songster of the grove;
No tree-enchanting Philomel
  To tell his tale of love.

There the industrious hand may toil,
  There cast the golden grain;
There Autumn's ample crop shall fail,
  There man will delve in vain.

For thou wilt baffle all his art
  As long as time shall flow,
And be that barren waste thou wert
  Ten thousand years ago.

**Robert Stephen Hawker 1803–1875**

## The Song of Western Men (Trelawny)[1]

A good sword and a trusty hand!
    A merry heart and true!
King James's men shall understand
    What Cornish lads can do.

And have they fixed the where and when?
    And shall Trelawny die?
Here's twenty thousand Cornish men
    Will know the reason why!

Out spake their captain brave and bold,
    A merry wight was he:
"If London Tower were Michael's hold,
    We'll set Trelawny free!"

"We'll cross the Tamar, land to land,
    The Severn is no stay,
With 'one and all', and hand in hand,
    And who shall bid us nay?"

"And when we come to London Wall,
    A pleasant sight to view,
Come forth! come forth, ye cowards all,
    Here's men as good as you!"

"Trelawny he's in the keep and hold,
    Trelawny he may die,
But here's twenty thousand Cornish bold,
    Will know the reason why!"


## The Sea[2]

I love the ocean! from a very child
  It has been to me as a nursing breast,
    Cherishing wild fancies. –

                     I was wont to rest
Gazing upon it, when the breeze was wild,
  And think that every wave reared its white arms
To grasp and chide the wind that rolled along

In fitful buffetings, chanting its hoarse song
   As in stern mockery! Such a scene had charms
For my young heart.

               And when the autumn moon
Laughed o'er the waters, it was mine to trace
   Her imagined form; as if her tiring-place
Were the wave's bosom, or seeking there some boon
   Of sea-god in his coral bower, she stayed,
Wronging Endymion – then the wind would cease,
And every murmur melt away in peace,
   And all be gentle as a softening maid
   Breathing love's tell-tale sigh.

              'Tis said
In such a night the daughters of the sea
Wake their wild harps in siren minstrelsy;
   And on their crystal-pillowed couches spread
Their clustering tresses, wooing the young breeze
   To wanton with their ringlets, or whispering tales
Of passionate homage to some chosen star,
Beautifully journeying in its azure car
Through paths of loveliness.

             Joys such as these,
   Visions of wayless fancy, were the fire
   That burnt within me, and they strung the lyre
My feeble hands have swept.


# The Silent Tower of Bottreau[3]

Tintadgel bells ring o'er the tide,
The boy leans on his vessel side;
He hears that sound, and dreams of home
Soothe the wild orphan of the foam.
     "Come to thy God in time!"
     Thus saith their pealing chime:
     Youth, manhood, old age past,
     "Come to thy God at last."

But why are Bottreau's echoes still?
Her tower stands proudly on the hill;
Yet the strange chough[4] that home hath found,
The lamb lies sleeping on the ground.
     "Come to thy God in time!"
     Should be her answering chime:

"Come to thy God at last!"
Should echo on the blast.

The ship rode down with courses free,
The daughter of a distant sea:
Her sheet was loose, her anchor stored,
The merry Bottreau bells on board.
    "Come to thy God in time!"
    Rung out Tintadgel chime;
    Youth, manhood, old age past,
    "Come to thy God at last!"

The pilot heard his native bells
Hang on the breeze in fitful swells;
"Thank God," with reverent brow he cried,
"We make the shore with evening's tide."
    "Come to thy God in time!"
    It was his marriage chime:
    Youth, manhood, old age past,
    His bell must ring at last.

"Thank God, thou whining knave, on land,
But thank, at sea, the steersman's hand,"
The captain's voice above the gale:
"Thank the good ship and ready sail."
    "Come to thy God in time!"
    Sad grew the boding chime:
    "Come to thy God at last!"
    Boomed heavy on the blast.

Uprose that sea! as if it heard
The mighty Master's signal-word:
What thrills the captain's whitening lip?
The death-groans of his sinking ship.
    "Come to thy God in time!"
    Swung deep the funeral chime:
    Grace, mercy, kindness past,
    "Come to thy God at last!"

Long did the rescued pilot tell –
When grey hairs o'er his forehead fell,
While those around would hear and weep –
That fearful judgment of the deep.
    "Come to thy God in time!"
    He read his native chime:
    Youth, manhood, old age past,
    His bell rung out at last.

Still when the storm of Bottreau's waves
Is wakening in his weedy caves:
Those bells, that sullen surges hide,
Peal their deep notes beneath the tide:
    "Come to thy God in time!"
    Thus saith the ocean chime:
    Storm, billow, whirlwind past,
    "Come to thy God at last!"


## The Western Shore

Thou lovely land! where, kindling, throng
Scenes that should breathe the soul of song;
Home of high hopes that once were mine
Of loftier verse and nobler line!

'Tis past – the quenched volcano's tide
Sleeps well within the mountain-side;
Henceforth shall time's cold touch control
The warring Hecla of my soul.

Welcome, wild rock and lonely shore!
Where round my days dark seas shall roar,
And thy grey fane, Morwenna,[5] stand
The beacon of the Eternal Land!


## The Poor Man and his Parish Church[6]

The poor have hands, and feet, and eyes,
   Flesh, and a feeling mind:
They breathe the breath of mortal sighs,
   They are of human kind.
They weep such tears as others shed,
   And now and then they smile: –
For sweet to them is that poor bread,
   They win with honest toil.

The poor men have their wedding-day:
   And children climb their knee:
They have not many friends, for they
   Are in such misery.
They sell their youth, their skill, their pains,
   For hire in hill and glen:

The very blood within their veins,
   It flows for other men.

They should have roofs to call their own,
   When they grow old and bent:
Meek houses built of dark grey stone,
   Worn labour's monument.
There should they dwell, beneath the thatch,
   With threshold calm and free:
No stranger's hand should lift the latch,
   To mark their poverty.

Fast by the church those walls should stand,
   Her aisles in youth they trod: –
They have no home in all the land,
   Like that old House of God.
There, there, the Sacrament was shed,
   That gave them heavenly birth;
And lifted up the poor man's head
   With princes of the earth.

There in the chancel's voice of praise,
   Their simple vows were poured;
And angels looked with equal gaze
   On Lazarus and his Lord.
There, too, at last, they calmly sleep,
   Where hallow'd blossoms bloom;
And eyes as fond and faithful weep
   As o'er the rich man's tomb.

They told me of an ancient home,
   Beside a churchyard wall,
Where roses round the porch would roam,
   And gentle jasmines fall:
There dwelt an old man, worn and blind,
   Poor, and of lowliest birth;
He seemed the last of all his kind –
   He had no friend on earth.

Men saw him till his eyes grew dim
   At morn and evening tide
Pass, 'mid the graves, with tottering limb,
   To the grey chancel's side:
There knelt he down, and meekly prayed
   The prayer his youth had known;
Words by the old Apostles made,
   In tongues of ancient tone.

At matin-time, at evening hour,
  He bent with reverent knee:
The dial carved upon the tower
  Was not more true than he.
This lasted till the blindness fell
  In shadows round his bed;
And on those walls he loved so well,
  He looked, and they were fled.

Then would he watch, and fondly turn,
  If feet of men were there,
To tell them how his soul would yearn
  For the old place of prayer;
And some would lead him on to stand,
  While fast their tears would fall,
Until he felt beneath his hand
  The long-accustomed wall.

Then joy in those dim eyes would melt;
  Faith found the former tone;
His heart within his bosom felt
  The touch of every stone.
He died – he slept beneath the dew,
  In his own grassy mound:
The corpse, within the coffin, knew
  That calm, that holy ground.

I know not why – but when they tell
  Of houses fair and wide,
Where troops of poor men go to dwell
  In chambers side by side: –
I dream of that old cottage door,
  With garlands overgrown,
And wish the children of the poor
  Had flowers to call their own.

And when they vaunt, that in those walls
  They have their worship day,
Where the stern signal coldly calls
  The prisoned poor to pray, –
I think upon that ancient home
  Beside the churchyard wall,
Where roses round the porch would roam,
  And gentle jasmines fall.

I see the old man of my lay,
  His grey head bowed and bare;
He kneels by one dear wall to pray,

The sunlight in his hair.
Well! they may strive, as wise men will,
   To work with wit and gold:
I think my own dear Cornwall still
   Was happier of old.

O! for the poor man's church again,
   With one roof over all;
Where the true hearts of Cornish men
   Might beat beside the wall:
The altars where, in holier days,
   Our fathers were forgiven,
Who went, with meek and faithful ways,
   Through the old aisles to heaven.


## Featherstone's Doom

Twist thou and twine! in light and gloom
   A spell in on thine hand;
The wind shall be thy changeful loom,
   Thy web the shifting sand.

Twine from this hour, in ceaseless toil,
   On Blackrock's[7] sullen shore;
Till cordage of the sand shall coil
   Where crested surges roar.

'Tis for that hour, when, from the wave,
   Near voices wildly cried;
When thy stern hand no succour gave,
   The cable at thy side.

Twist thou and twine! in light and gloom
   The spell is on thine hand;
The wind shall be thy changeful loom,
   The web the shifting sand.


## The Figure-Head[8] of the "Caledonia" at her Captain's Grave

We laid them in their lowly rest,
   The strangers of a distant shore;
We smoothed the green turf on their breast,
   'Mid baffled Ocean's angry roar;

And there, the relique of the storm,
We fixed fair Scotland's figured form.

She watches by her bold, her brave,
  Her shield towards the fatal sea:
Their cherished lady of the wave
  Is guardian of their memory.
Stern is her look, but calm, for there
No gale can rend or billow bear.

Stand, silent image! stately stand,
  Where sighs shall breathe and tears be shed,
And many a heart of Cornish land,
  Will soften for the stranger dead.
They came in paths of storm; they found
This quiet home in Christian ground.


# Sir Beville[9] – The Gate-Song of Stowe

Arise! and away! for the King and the land;
  Farewell to the couch and the pillow:
With spear in the rest, and with rein in the hand,
  Let us rush on the foe like a billow.

Call the hind from the plough, and the herd from the fold,
  Bid the wassailer cease from his revel:
And ride for old Stowe, where the banner's unrolled,
  For the cause of King Charles and Sir Beville.

Trevanion is up, and Godolphin is nigh,
  And Harris of Hayne's o'er the river;
From Lundy to Looe, "One and All" is the cry,
  And the King and Sir Beville for ever.

Ay! by Tre, Pol, and Pen, ye may know Cornish men,
  'Mid the names and the nobles of Devon; –
But if truth to the King be a signal, why then
  Ye can find out the Granville in heaven.

Ride! ride! with red spur, there is death in delay,
  'Tis a race for dear life with the devil;
If dark Cromwell prevail, and the King must give way,
  This earth is no place for Sir Beville.

So at Stamford he fought, and at Lansdown he fell,
   But vain were the visions he cherished:
For the great Cornish heart, that the King loved so well,
   In the grave of the Granville it perished.


# Modryb Marya[10] – Aunt Mary

Now of all the trees by the king's highway,
      Which do you love the best?
O! the one that is green upon Christmas Day,
      The bush with the bleeding breast.
Now the holly with her drops of blood for me:
For that is our dear Aunt Mary's tree.

Its leaves are sweet with our Saviour's Name,
      'Tis a plant that loves the poor:
Summer and winter it shines the same,
      Beside the cottage door.
O! the holly with her drops of blood for me:
For that is our kind Aunt Mary's tree.

'Tis a bush that the birds will never leave:
      They sing in it all day long;
But sweetest of all upon Christmas Eve,
      Is to hear the robin's song.
'Tis the merriest sound upon earth and sea:
For it comes from our own Aunt Mary's tree.

So, of all that grows by the king's highway,
      I love that tree the best;
'Tis a bower for the birds upon Christmas Day,
      The bush of the bleeding breast.
O! the holly with her drops of blood for me:
For that is our sweet Aunt Mary's tree.


# The Cornish Emigrant's Song

Oh! the eastern winds are blowing;
   The breezes seem to say,
'We are going, we are going,
   To North Americay.

'There the merry bees are humming
   Around the poor man's hive;

Parson Kingdon is not coming
  To take away their tithe.

'There the yellow corn is growing
  Free as the king's highway;
So we're going, we are going,
  To North Americay.

'Uncle Rab shall be churchwarden,
  And Dick shall be the squire,
And Jem, that lived at Norton,
  Shall be leader of the quire;

'And I will be the preacher,
  And preach three times a day
To every living creature
  In North Americay.'

## The Tamar Spring[11]

Fount of a rushing river! wild flowers wreathe
  The home where thy first waters sunlight claim;
The lark sits hushed beside thee, while I breathe,
  Sweet Tamar spring! the music of thy name.

On! through the goodly channel, on! to the sea!
  Pass amid heathery vale, tall rock, fair bough:
But never more with footsteps pure and free,
  Or face so meek with happiness as now.

Fair is the future scenery of thy days,
  Thy course domestic, and thy paths of pride:
Depths that give back the soft-eyed violet's gaze,
  Shores where tall navies march to meet the tide.

Thine, leafy Tetcott, and those neighbouring walls,
  Noble Northumberland's embowered domain;
Thine, Cartha Martha, Morwell's rocky falls,
  Storied Cotehele, and Ocean's loveliest plain.

Yet false the vision, and untrue the dream,
  That lures thee from thy native wilds to stray:
A thousand griefs will mingle with that stream,
  Unnumbered hearts shall sigh those waves away.

Scenes fierce with men, thy seawards current laves,
  Harsh multitudes will throng thy gentle brink;
Back with the grieving concourse of thy waves,
  Home to the waters of thy childhood shrink.

Thou heedest not! thy dream is of the shore,
  Thy heart is quick with life; on! to the sea!
How will the voice of thy far streams implore
  Again amid these peaceful weeds to be!

My soul! my soul! a happier choice be thine –
  Thine is the hushed valley, and the lonely sod;
False dreams, far vision, hollow hope resign,
  Fast by our Tamar spring, alone with God!

## The Storm

War, 'mid the ocean and the land!
The battlefield, Morwenna's strand,
Where rock and ridge the bulwark keep,
The giant-warders of the deep.

They come! and shall they not prevail,
The seething surge, the gathering gale?
They fling their wild flag to the breeze,
The banner of a thousand seas.

They come – they mount – they charge in vain,
Thus far, incalculable main!
No more! thine hosts have not o'erthrown
The lichen on the barrier stone.

Have the rocks faith, that thus they stand,
Unmoved, a grim and stately band,
And look, like warriors tried and brave,
Stern, silent, reckless, o'er the wave?

Have the proud billows thought and life,
To feel the glory of the strife;
And trust, one day, in battle bold,
To win the foeman's haughty hold?

Mark where they writhe with pride and shame,
Fierce valour, and the zeal of fame!
Hear how their din of madness raves,
The baffled army of the waves!

Thy way, O God, is in the sea,
Thy paths, where awful waters be;
Thy Spirit thrills the conscious stone:
O Lord, Thy footsteps are not known!


# A Croon on Hennacliff[12]

Thus said the rushing raven,
  Unto his hungry mate:
"Ho! gossip! for Bude Haven:
  There be corpses six or eight.
Cawk! cawk! the crew and skipper
  Are wallowing in the sea:
So there's a savoury supper
  For my old dame and me."

"Cawk! gaffer! thou art dreaming
  The shore hath wreckers bold;
Would rend the yelling seamen,
  From the clutching billows' hold.
Cawk! cawk! they'd bound for booty
  Into the dragon's den:
And shout, for 'death or duty,'
  If the prey were drowning men."

Loud laughed the listening surges,
  At the guess our grandame gave:
You might call them Boanerges,
  From the thunder of their wave.
And mockery followed after
  The sea-bird's jeering brood:
That filled the skies with laughter,
  From Lundy Light to Bude.

"Cawk! cawk!" then said the raven,
  "I am fourscore years and ten:
Yet never in Bude Haven,
  Did I croak for rescued men. –
They will save the Captain's girdle,
  And shirt, if shirt there be:
But leave their blood to curdle,
  For my old dame and me."

So said the rushing raven,
  Unto his hungry mate:
"Ho! gossip! for Bude Haven:
  There be corpses six or eight.

Cawk! cawk! the crew and skipper
  Are wallowing in the sea:
O what a savoury supper
  For my old dame and me."


# The Fatal Ship[13]

Down the deep sea! full fourscore fathoms down!
  An iron vault hath clutched five hundred men!
They died not, like the nations, one by one:
  A thrill! a bounding pulse! a shout! and then
  Five hundred hearts stood still, at once, nor beat again!

That night the Angel of the Lord beheld
  A vast battalion of the gliding dead:
Souls that came up where seething surges quelled
  Their stately ship – their throne – and now the bed
  Where they shall wait, in shrouded sleep, the Morn of Dread!

Fast slept the sailor-boy! A silent dream
  Soften'd his brow with smiles – his mother's face
Droops over him – and her soft kisses seem
  Warm on his cheek: what severs that embrace?
  Death! strangling death! – alive – a conscious burial-place!

And he, the kingly mind, whose skill had planned
  That lordly bastion of the world of waves?
But yesterday he stood, in proud command,
  And now a thing of nought, where ocean raves
  Above his shuddering sepulchre in the weedy caves!

The monsters of the sea will glide and glare:
  Baffled Leviathan shall roar in vain:
The Sea Kings of the Isles are castled there:
  They man that silent fortress of the main:
  Yea! in the realms of death their dust shall rule and reign!

Lord Yahvah,[14] of the Waters! Thou wert there!
  Thy presence shone throughout that dark abode:
Thy mighty touch assuaged the last despair:
  Their pulses paused in the calm midst of God:
  Their souls, amid surrounding Angels, went abroad!

# The Doom-Well of St Madron[15]

"Plunge thy right hand in St Madron's spring,
If true to its troth be the palm you bring:
But if a false sigil thy fingers bear,
Lay them the rather on the burning share."

Loud laughed King Arthur whenas he heard
That solemn friar his boding word:
And blithly he sware as a king he may
"We tryst for St Madron's at break of day."

"Now horse and hattock, both but and ben,"[16]
With the cry at Lauds, with Dundagel men;
And forth they pricked upon Routorr[17] side,
As goodly a raid as a king could ride.

Proud Gwennivar rode like a queen of the land,
With page and with squire at her bridle hand;
And the twice six knights of the stony ring,
They girded and guarded their Cornish king.

Then they halted their steeds at St Madron's cell:
And they stood by the monk of the cloistered well;
"Now off with your gauntlets," King Arthur he cried
"And glory or shame for our Tamar side."

'Twere sooth to sing how Sir Gauvain smiled,
When he grasped the waters so soft and mild;
How Sir Lancelot dashed the glistening spray
O'er the rugged beard of the rough Sir Kay.

Sir Bevis he touched and he found no fear:
Twas a bénité stoup to Sir Belvidere,
How the fountain flashed o'er King Arthur's Queen
Say, Cornish dames, for ye guess the scene.

"Now rede me my riddle, Sir Mordred, I pray,
My kinsman, mine ancient, my bien-aimé;
Now rede me my riddle, and rede it aright,
Art thou knave or my trusty knight?"

He plunged his right arm in the judgement well,
It bubbled and boiled like a cauldron of hell:
He drew and he lifted his quivering limb,
Ha! Sir Judas, how Madron had sodden him!

Now let Uter Pendragon do what he can,
Still the Tamar river will run as it ran:
Let King or let Kaiser be fond or be fell,
Ye may harowe their troth in St Madron's well.

**Robert Hunt 1807–1887**

## *From* The Mount's Bay

"Who gazes on yon holy place,
Whose tower is marbled with the trace
Of centuries which have past away,
Sowing the cankers of decay.

...............................................

On Landewednack's[1] sacred pile,
And gives it not a passing smile?
A smile of reverence and awe,
To think how well it stands the blow;
To view that holy, aged state,
Which all who feel, must venerate.
But if it be the tourist's mood
To seek for a sublimer food;
Or from canzonel releas'd
The bard would seek a nobler feast;
'Tis found magnificently deep,
At Kynance Cove, whose awful steep
In terror lives, and on the shore
We hear a new Charybidis' roar;
Whose voice is as the thunder loud,
When bursting from the direful cloud,
Its wrath is hurl'd upon the land;
And ravages on either hand,
A vast pneumatic engine wrought
By powers too great for common thought.
Or traveller...
                    ...would you seek to see
The beetling rocks immensity;
Mount them and cast your eyes below;
Thrilling the strong electric blow
Which all must feel, when from such height
They gaze on depths, majestic might.

...............................................

Though a Cimmerian[2] darkness dwells
Upon the Lizard's moss grown dells;
Bare of the robes which verdure gives
Spots where alone Disorder lives...

...............................................

'Tis sweet to see the varied hue,
More chequer'd than e'en painter drew,
That decks the wild and frowning moor,

114

And coronets the angry shore.
There spreads the Deep unto the bound,
Where the horizon chains it round;
Here we may view a fertile glade
And there the ivied crag's dark shade;
Here stands a temple built for prayer,
A cottage and a garden there –
Here do we catch the streamlet's sigh,
A rapid torrent there sweeps by.
But let us on our fruitful rounds
Traverse across Goonhilly Downs;
Where sweet Erica lifts her head,
In wildness of profusion spread;
Rising around in truant play
Soothing the dark and dreary way,
To where Gunwalloe's aged fane,
In lonely mood, and lowly mien,
Is shadowed by the rising hill,
Where all is dreary, all is still.
No sound wakes Echo from her cave,
Saving the murmur of the wave;
But in this waste how sweet to see,
A place to worship Deity!"

**Henry Sewell Stokes 1808–1895**

## The Lady of Place[1]

Five hundred years and more ago,
  Third Edward ruled us then,
From Fowey near fifty ships set sail,
  With nigh eight hundred men:
No other Port on England's coast
  An equal force could bring;
For Calais when they weigh'd, they form'd
  The Vanguard of the King.

And when Henries reign'd the Sixth,
  The ships of Fowey went forth
To every sea, and every shore,
  East, West, and South, and North;
And the Bay was like a forest
  For tall and stately masts,
And flags of many countries
  Came with the veering blasts.

The Fowey men grew so haughty,
  They would no bonnet veil;
But the folk of Rye and Winchelsea
  Would make them dip the sail.
And on a day, to settle it,
  They fought both man and boy;
And from that time those Cornish lads
  Were called Gallants of Fowey.

Still more they fell to merchandise,
  And prouder still did grow:
Their cruisers harass'd all the coast
  From Cherbourg to Bordeaux.
But one dark night, when scatter'd far
  Their ships on Ocean wide,
A sound as from a cloud of sails
  Came with the flowing tide.

The Lady of Treffry remain'd
  In her large mansion lone;
Her husband to the distant chase
  With horse and hounds had gone.
The watch-dogs bark'd; then shouts – then shrieks
  Rose from the sleeping town;
The vengeful French, like unloosed fiends,
  Went ranging up and down.

Here torches flash'd, there sledges crash'd,
    Such was their devilish game;
And soon from many a house-top
    Burst out the crimson flame.
As in broad day men saw the bay,
    The ships, the shores, the towers;
Then blinding clouds of smoke came down,
    And red flakes fell in showers.

But she was there, that Lady,
    To play no woman's part;
Though the great sufferings of her town
    Had pierced her gentle heart:
And Fowey men, like a wall of steel,
    Though few, about her stood;
While some, to cut the ships adrift,
    Crept out upon the flood.

And on the wharves, and in the streets,
    Was heard the awful clang
Of swords and weapons strange; with fists
    Some on the Frenchman sprang;
Some met them with a Cornish grip
    They never more forgot;
And many found the Cornish hug[2]
    Much rougher than they thought.

But other were the scenes and sounds
    Of that unhappy night,
When, like a flock of bleating lambs,
    By the burning roof-trees' light,
Mothers their wailing children led
    Through wood and shelter'd lane,
And up the winding moorland paths
    Which to this day remain.

Still calm look'd forth the Lady
    From her embattled wall;
Her presence was a power, her voice
    Thrill'd like a trumpet's call.
Meanwhile the bells kept tolling,
    To rouse the country round;
And spires and turrets far away
    Sent on the warning sound.

And long before the daylight
    Fires lit the lofty peaks;
And men were moving in the vales,

And stirring in the creeks.
Small need – so brave that Lady proved,
    The Fowey gallants so true,
That at cock-crow, like baffled wolves,
    The Frenchmen all withdrew.

Whether a panic seized them,
    I will not pause to learn;
They had done enough of mischief,
    And might perhaps return.
But, when they went to find their ships,
    The Fowey folk laugh'd outright;
For some were scuttled, some aground,
    Some drifting out of sight.

Next morning with his Posse
    The Sheriff came at dawn;
The flames still roar'd, the French on board
    The ships they saved had gone:
Three cheers, then, for the Fowey gallants!
    For the Lady three times three!
And, if the French should come again,
    May our wives as fearless be!

Changed is the world, much changed since then,
    Yet will they come once more?
Who knows – or cares – or fears? who doubts
    We'll serve them as before?
Grace Darling[3] died but yesterday,
    And others of her race
May yet be found to emulate
    That brave Lady of Place.

# Life

Describe me life. A blossom'd thorn,
A poppy waving in the corn,
Waiting the silent reaper's thrust, –
A bubble's shadow, dreams and dust.

Give me some other similes,
The thistle-down before the breeze,
A leaf, a flower, a bead of dew,
A gossamer – what more would you?

Your fancy's fertile – try again
'Tis a steed bounding on the plain,
'Tis a sail scudding from the strand,
A bird, a wave, a drift of sand.

Can you no other symbols find?
A cadence wafted on the wind,
The fitful breathing of a shell,
The echo of a plaintive bell.

**Charles Chorley 1810–1874**

# What Constitutes a Mine?

What constitutes a mine?
Not agent's house, nor ornate counting-house,
  Where bold adventurers dine;
Not shops where carpenter his art may use,
  And smith his brawny arm;
Not stable nor material-house or mill,
  Nor shed to shield from the storm.
Nor floods, nor powder-house, nor useful rill;
  No – ore, deep-treasured ore,
Of power the adventurous foreigner to lure
  O'er many a hill and moor,
Sustained by hope rich profits to ensure;
  Ore – copper, tin, or lead.
With well-sunk shaft, and ladder, lift, and beam;
  And above all, is need
Of engine moved by wonder-working steam.
  These constitute a mine;
And parish officers in vain debate,
  And lawyers cute combine,
Aught among these by sessions low to rate,
  Counselled by statesmen sage,
When England's maiden-queen, in prudence great,
  Made low for pauper age,
Mines she exempted from the parish rate.
  Such was her parish law,
And nought were fairer for Cornubia's weal.
  Shall farmers then o'erawe?
Or lawyers threaten us that laws repeal?
  Since mines so rarely pay
Those sweet rewards we labour to ensure,
  'Tis folly to give way
And pay unmurmuring to the parish poor.

## William Bentinck Forfar 1810–1895

# The Bal, or, 'Tes a Bra' Keenly Lode

If you'll listen to me for a moment, you shall
Hear all about trying and working a Bal;[1]
How the Lode is discovered by a small hazel twig,
Carried over the ground by some knowing old prig,
Who knows when his Dowzing has answered its end,
For wherever the Lode is the hazel will bend:
But when these mystical rites are performed in the night,
The Lode's sometimes discovered by a Phospheric Light.[2]
     Aw! 'tes a Bra' Keenly Lode,
     Aw! 'tes a Bra' Keenly Lode.

When the knowing old Dowzer this discovery's made
He marks out the spot and then calls his comrade,
Saying, "Hallo! Cozen Jan, d'ee come 'long wi' me,
'Tes the keenliest gozan[3] thee ever ded'st see;
Wi' my pick an' my gad I've ben worken oal night,
An' a g'eat piece of mundic[4] es jest heaved in sight."
"Aw! ef that es the caase, then," says Jan, "I'll be bound
Weth a few hours' worken, the lode'll be found."
     Aw! 'tes a Bra' Keenly Lode,
     Aw! 'tes a Bra' Keenly Lode.

When they came to the Lode, then the water came in,
And they couldn't tell whether 'twas copper or tin.
"Come," says Jan, "lev es go to the kiddle-e-wink,[5]
An' set down, touch our pipes, and ha' sumthen to drink,
An' to-morraw we'll call upon Cap'n Polglaaze,
An' ax hes advice, when we've laid forth our caase.
He do knaw some rich chaps up to Lunnon, I'm towld.
*So he can promise our tin in exchange for their gowld."*
     Aw! 'tes a Bra' Keenly Lode,
     Aw! 'tes a Bra' Keenly Lode.

Now Captain Polglaaze was a purser, well known,
Who quickly, by mining, a rich man had grown:
So he sampled the ore which the two men brought him;
And advised them, by all means, to put up a whim,
And to fork out the water with a pump and a wheel,
While he to his friends would make instant appeal;
And to London he'd go with a sample of ore:–
"Loar!" says Jan, "I shud liek to go weth ee, plaise sure."
     Aw! 'tes a Bra' Keenly Lode,
     Aw! 'tes a Bra' Keenly Lode.

They went up to Bristol by a steamer from Hayle,
And proceeded from Bristol to London by rail,
And, having finished their business without much delay
They came back to Cornwall again, the same way.
And when they returned to their comrades again,
They were looked upon more like "g'eat anjuls" than men.
They met that same night, – Cousin Jan took the chair, –
And then his adventures he told to the *Pair.*

  Aw! 'tes a Bra' Keenly Lode,
  Aw! 'tes a Bra' Keenly Lode.


## A Dialogue between Gracey Penrose and Mally Treviskey

*Gracey*
Fath and trath then I b'lieve in ten parishes round
Sichey rogue, suchey vellan, es not to be found!

*Mally*
What's the fussing Un' Gracey, long wetha, cheeld vean?

*Gracey*
A fussing, aketha! od splet es ould brain, –
Our Martin's come hum cheeld so drunk as a baist,
So cross as the gallish from Perranzan vaist,[6]
A kicking, a tottering, a cussing, and swearing,
So hard as the stompses[7] a tarving and tearing.

*Mally*
Never mind it Un Gracey, – cheeld, put un to bed;
He'll slaip oal the liquor away from his head.

*Gracey*
I wudden go neast un to fang the king's crown
For a swears ef I spaik t'un, he'll cleave my skull down.
Thee never in all thy born days, fath and shure,
Dedst behould sich a maazedgerry[8] pattick afore;
Why a scat all to midjans[9] and jouds[10] for the nons,
A cloam buzz[11] of scale milk about on the scons;
And a catched up a shoul for toe steave[12] me outright,
But I runned away ready to fainty for fright.
Do tell me, Un Mally! what shall I do by un –
For zountikins! death! I'm affeared to go nigh un.

*Mally*

I knaw what I'd gee'n, ef so be 'twere my case,
I'd scat the ould chacks un, I'd trem un, Un Grace.

*Gracey*

I'm affeard a my life to go nigh the ould vellan:
Else, plaise faather, I b'lieve I should parfectly kill un,
But I'll never no more be so baald and abused;
My arms here like bazam, the rogue have abruised!
I maade for hes supper a muggetty pie;
But a shaan't clunk a croom o't, I wish he may die.

*Mally*

I tould thee afore that the job was a done,
That theedst come to repent it so sure as a gun,
But thee wusn't hark to me, for doubting for why,
Becaase thee dedst knaw un much better than I.
But I knawed the trem un before thee hadst got un,
And tould thee a mashes of stories about un.
But thee answered so toytish, and shrinked up tha noze,
A gissing 'twas great stramming lies I suppose.
There's waun of his pranks I shall always remember,
('Twill be dree years agone come the 'ighth of November),
I'd tow purty young mabyers as eyes could behould,
So fat as the butter, just 'ighteen weeks ould:
They were picking about in the town-plaace for mait,
So I hove down some pellas among em' to ait,
When who but your man come a tottering along,
So drunk that I thoft he would faall in the dung;
A left faall his hobban-bag jest by the door,
So I caalled to the man, as waun would to be sure:
Says I, "Martin! dost heer, cheeld? come take up the bag."
"Arra (sez a) for what art a scaling me, dog?"
And runned vore towards me, nor better nor wuss,
Knacked the maybers both steff with a dail more of fuss.
Like enow ef I hadn't got hasties away,
He'd adone as ded by Jan Rose t' other day;
When a got in his tantrums, a wilful ould devil,
And slammed the poor man in the head with a kebbal.

*Gracey*

When the cyder is runned away every drap,
'Tes too laate to be thinken of pluggin' the tap;
And marriage must go as the Loard doth ordain;
Yet ef I'd knawed the coose un, Un Mally, cheeld vean!
Ef I'd knawed the coose un but nine weeks ago,
I'd never a had the ould vellan, I knaw,
But a vowed and a sweared that ef I'd be hes wife,

I never should want all the days of my life;
And broft me a nackin and corn-saive from Preen –
In ma conscience, thoft I, I shall live like a queen!
But 'tes plaguey provoking, ad splet hes ould head;
To be pooted and slopt so, I wish a wor dead:
Why a spent haaf hes fangings laast Saturday night,
Like, enow, by this time, 'tes gone every doit;
But I'll taame the ould devil afore et es long –
Ef I caan't wi' ma vistes, I will wi' ma tongue!

**John Harris 1820–1884**

## *From* Christian Heroism[1]

Hast ever seen a mine? Has ever been
Down in its fabled grottoes, walled with gems,
And canopied with torrid mineral belts,
That blaze within the fiery orifice?
Hast ever, by the glimmer of the lamp,
Or the fast-waning taper, gone down, down,
Towards the earth's dread centre, where wise men
Have told us that the earthquake is conceived,
And great Vesuvius hath his lava-house,
Which burns and burns for ever, shooting forth
As from a fountain of eternal fire?
Hast ever heard, within this prison-house,
The startling hoof of Fear? the eternal flow
Of some dread meaning whispering to thy soul?
Hast ever seen the miner at his toil,
Following his obscure work below, below,
Where not a single sun-ray visits him.
But all is darkness and perpetual night?
Here the dull god of gloom unrivalled reigns,
And wraps himself in palls of pitchy dark!
Hast ever breathed its sickening atmosphere?
Heard its dread throbbings, when the rock has burst?
Leaped at its sneezings in the powder-blast?
And trembled when the groaning, splitting earth,
Mass after mass, fell down with deadliest crash?
What sayest thou? – thou hast not? – Come with me;
Or if thou hast, no matter, come again.
Don't fear to trust me; for I have been there
From morn till night, from night till dewy morn,
Gasping within its burning sulphur-cloud,
Straining mine eyes along its ragged walls,
And wondering at the uncouth passages
Dashed in the sparry cells by Fancy's wand;
And oft have paused, and paused again, to hear
The eternal echo of its emptiness.

Come, let us leave the fields and flowers behind,
The murmuring brooklet where the poet walks,
Weaving life's cobwebs into silken flowers
To beautify the homes of fatherland.
Come, let us leave the beauteous light of day,
The bower of roses, and the Muses' haunt,
Where the green ivy roofs us overhead;
And go down, down, into the earth's black breast,

Where, in the bottom of a shaft, two men
Prepare e'en now to blast the solid rock.
The hole is bored; the powder is confined;
The fuse is fixed, – it cannot be drawn forth.
They negligently cut it with a stone
Against a rod of iron. Fire is struck!
The fuse is hissing: and they fly, both fly,
Towards the bucket, taking hold thereon,
Shrieking the well-known signal. He above
Strove, but in vain, to put the windlass round.
One could escape, – delay was death to both!
One of them was our hero. Stepping back,
He looked a moment in his comrade's face, –
O what a look was that! – and cried, "Escape!
A minute more, and I shall be heaven."
On sped the bucket up the sounding shaft:
The man was safe! Eager to watch his fate,
The fate of his deliverer, down he stoop'd,
And bent him o'er the shaft, just when the roar
Of the explosion rumbled from below.
Up came a fragment of the rifted rock,
And struck him on the brow, leaving a mark.
Which tells him still of his deliverance,
A mark which Time will never chip away
With his rough hatchet, but it will remain
Till Death shall wrap him in his murky pall!

They soon began, among the fallen rock,
To burrow for the corpse. At last they heard
A cheering voice – the voice of him their friend –
Ring in the rattling fragments! Here he was,
Roofed over with the rock, – alive and well!
Forth from his fearful grave the hero came,
And smiled on all around him. Daniel's God
Had saved His servant in this dangerous hour.
All he could tell was, that, when left alone,
He sat down in a corner of the shaft,
And held a piece of rock before his eyes,
To wait the issue. And when asked why he
Gave up his life to save his friend, he said,
"His little children would be wet with grief,
While I had none but my sudden death to mourn."

## *From* The Mine

Meanwhile the mine extended and grew rich,
And every month the workmen multiplied;
The water gushed from countless cracks unseen,
Ran down the levels' sides, and bubbled up
Within the adit,[2] keeping the bold men
From sinking far beneath it, till the wheel
Was laid aside, and in its place arose
A small steam-engine newly wonderful;
And wonderful the ease with which it wrought,
Draining the mine as strangely as a spell.
After the shaft was sixty feet in depth,
Ends were extended eastward, westward far;
Then winzes[3] sunk for air from level to level;
And so it ever was and ever is.
And as they sunk from rugged stair to stair,
The troubled entrails of the rifled world
Changed hard as marble. Drills were introduced,
And mallets rang where picks had clinked before.
Then holes were blasted in a dangerous way,
By rushes thrust into the powder-charge
Through a small hole made by a copper wire,
Igniting it as sudden as a thought;
Ere the poor wretch could say one word of prayer,
Destroying limbs and often life itself.
Then quills were used. Still very dangerous they
And more expensive. Lastly came the fuse,
Unparalleled for safety. Turn we from the fields,
And ladder after ladder quick descend,
Until we reach a labourer's working-place.
It is the hour of morning: on a plank
A father and his elder son sit down,
A boy with fourteen Aprils on his face,
With thought of home and brothers in his mind,
And sunny slopes and lawns of laughing flowers,
Denied him here, denied the lad so soon.
A flask of water dangles to a nail,
And here a can of powder; candles there,
A pair of scissors, and a bunch of quills.
Their dinners lie beside them, and beyond
Are drills and hammers and long iron bars.
Ere they begin to labour, child and sire
Kneel down among the rocks, and that dark cave
Is visited by angels, whose bright wings
Float through the darkness to the voice of prayer.

...............................................................

Years stole away; the rich mine richer grew;
Another lode was added richer still:
It strangely shot out in the engine-shaft,
And so he hailed it as a friend with gems,
Who came to pour the treasures in his lap.
It was a vein of copper bright as brass,
Which soon became the theme at every hearth.
Copper has colours different in the ores,
As various as the rainbow – black and blue
And green and red and yellow as a flower;
Gold-coloured here, there dimly visible,
Though rich the same in measure and in meed.
'Tis found alike where glittering granite gloams,
Where killas[4] darkens, and where gossans shroud
And oft where wise ones write it cannot be –
Thus wisely scattered by the Hand Divine.
Tin is more secret far, with duller eye
Oft hiding in the river's shingly bed,
Or the flint's bosom, near the central fires,
In chambers wide, or veins like silken lace,
So that the labourer, stumbling on a start,[5]
Wipes his hot brow, and cries, 'Lo, here is tin.'

....................................................................

A mine spread out its vast machinery.
Here engines with their huts and smoky stacks,
Cranks, wheels, and rods, boilers and hissing steam.
Pressed up the water from the depths below.
Here fire-whims ran till almost out of breath,
And chains cried sharply, strained with fiery force.
Here blacksmiths hammered by the sooty forge,
And there a crusher crashed the copper ore.
Here girls were cobbing under roofs of straw,
And there were giggers[6] at the oaken hutch.
Here a man-engine glided up and down,
A blessing and a boon to mining men:
And near the spot, where many years before,
Turned round and round the rude old water wheel,
A huge fire-stamps was working evermore,
And slimy boys were swarming at the trunks.
The noisy lander[7] by the trap-door bawled
With pincers in his hand; and troops of maids
With heavy hammers brake the mineral stones.
The cart-man cried, and shook his broken whip;
And on the steps of the account-house stood
The active agent, with his eye on all.

Below were caverns grim with greedy gloom,
And levels drunk with darkness; chambers huge
Where Fear sat silent, and the mineral-sprite[8]
For-ever chanted his bewitching song;
Shafts deep and dreadful, looking darkest things
And seeming almost running down to doom;
Rock under foot, rock standing on each side;
Rock cold and gloomy, frowning overhead;
Before; behind, at every angle, rock.
Here blazed a vein of precious copper ore,
Where lean men laboured with a zeal for fame,
With face and hands and vesture black as night,
And down their sides the perspiration ran
In steaming eddies, sickening to behold.
But they complained not, digging day and night,
And morn and eve, with lays upon their lips.
Here yawned a tin-cell like a cliff of crags,
And Danger lurked among the groaning rocks,
And ofttimes moaned in darkness. All the air
Was black with sulphur and burning up the blood.
A nameless mystery seemed to fill the void,
And wings all pitchy flapped among the flints,
And eyes that saw not sparkled mid the spars.[9]
Yet here men worked, on stages hung in ropes,
With drills and hammers blasting the rude earth,
Which fell with such a crash that he who heard
Cried, "Jesu, save the miner!" Here were ends
Cut through hard marble by the miners' skill,
And winzes, stopes[10] and rizes:[11] pitches here,
Where worked the heroic, princely tributer,[12]
This month for nothing, next for fifty pounds.
Here lodes ran wide, and there so very small
That scarce a pick-point could be pressed between;
Here making walls as smooth as polished steel,
And there as craggy as a rended hill:
And out of sparry vagues the water oozed,
Staining the rock with mineral, so that oft
It led the labourer to a house of gems.
Across the mine a hollow cross-course ran
From north to south, an omen of much good;
And tin lay heaped on stulls[13] and level-plots;
And in each nook a tallow taper flared,
Where pale men wasted with exhaustion huge.
Here holes exploded, and there mallets rang,
And rocks fell crashing, lifting the stiff hair
From time-worn brows, and noisy buckets roared
In echoing shafts; and through this gulf of gloom
A hollow murmur rushed for evermore.

# On the Death of my Daughter Lucretia[14]

And art thou gone so soon?
And is thy loving gentle spirit fled?
Ah! is my fair, my passing beautiful,
My loved Lucretia numbered with the dead?
  Ah! art thou gone so soon?

  I miss thee, daughter, now,
In the dear nooks of earth we oft have trod
And a strange longing fills my yearning soul
To sleep with thee, and be, like thee, with God!
  I miss thee, daughter, now.

  I miss thee at thy books,
Lisping sweet Bible-accents in my ear,
Showing me pictures by the evening lamp,
Beautiful emblems thou didst love so dear:
  I miss thee at thy books.

  I miss thee at thy prayers,
When the eve-star is looking through the sky,
And thy lone sister kneels in sorrow down,
To pray to her great Father up on high:
  I miss thee at thy prayers.

  I miss thee by the brook,
Where we have wander'd many a summer's day,
And thou wert happy with thy loving sire,
More happy here than at thy simple play:
  I miss thee by the brook.

  I miss thee in the Reenes,[15]
Where we have hasted in the twilight dim
To wake the echoes of the silent dell,
And mark the glow-worm 'neath the hawthorn's limb:
  I miss thee in the Reenes.

  I miss thee on the Hill,
The dear old hill which we have climb'd so oft:
And O, how very happy have we been
In the still bower of the old heathy croft!
  I miss thee on the Hill.

  I miss thee at day's close,
When from my labour I regain my cot,
And sit down sadly at the supper-board,

Looking for thee, but, ah! I see thee not:
  I miss thee at day's close.

  I miss thee everywhere, –
In my small garden, watching the first flower, –
By the clear fountain, – in thy Sunday-class, –
Running to meet me at the evening hour:
  I miss thee everywhere.

  Farewell, my beautiful!
Thy sinless spirit is with Christ above:
Thou hast escaped the evils of the world:
We have a daughter in the meads of love.
  Farewell, my beautiful!

  When I and little Jane,
Walk hand in hand along the old hill's way,
Shall we not feel thy cherub-presence, love,
Singing our sad psalms in the twilight grey?
  I soon shall go to thee.

  Companion of the bard,
Mid rocks and trees, and hedges ivy-cross'd!
At morn and eve in Nature's presence-cell
We oft have enter'd with our musings lost,
  My child, my harp, and I.

  How thou didst love the flowers,
The mountain-heather and the buds of Spring,
The brooks and birds, the hush of solitude,
The moon and stars, like some diviner thing,
  Beautiful prophetess!

  Ah! thou wert like a rose,
Dropp'd by an angel on earth's feverish clime,
To bloom full lovely, till December winds
Blasted thy beauty in its morning's prime,
  Ere it had half unclosed!

  Hush, murmuring spirit, hush!
It is the Lord, He only, who hath given:
And He hath taken – blessed be His name! –
The gem, which fell from paradise, to heaven:
  I bow and kiss His rod.

## *From* Monro[16]

The heat, the cold, the sulphur and the slime,
  The grinding masses of the loosened rock,
The scaling ladders, the incessant grime
  From the dark timbers and the dripping block,
The lassitude, the mallet's frequent knock,
  The pain of thirst when water was so near,
The aching joints, the blasted hole's rude shock,
  Could not dash out the music from his ear,
Or stay the sound of song which ever murmured clear.

The cavern's sides, the vagues of shining spar,
  The roof of rock where scarce the candle gleams,
The hollow levels strangely stretching far
  Beneath the mountains, full of mineral seams,
Were evermore to him befitting themes,
  For meditation and his rustic lay;
While in the darkness his pale visage gleams,
  To read rich sonnets on the furrowed clay,
And craggy slabs that jut the ladder's lonely way.


## *From* A Story of Carn Brea[17]

How the great mountain like a rocky king
Stands silent in the tempest! Not a gust
With water laden, rushing with fierce front
Against his wrinkles, but he shakes it off,
Like filmy atoms from an insect's wing.
The thunder growls upon his splinter'd head,
Yelling from cave to cave, and every crag,
Carved by the Druid in the olden time,
When men were wont to worship on his crest,
Seems like a fiery pillar, as the flames
Leap from the clouds, and lick their knotty sides.
He, awful in his calmness, shakes his locks,
And gazes up into the solemn sky,
As if a strain of music shook the air.
O wondrous mountain, 'neath thy ribs of rock
Lie beds of precious mineral, which, when Time
With tardy feet hath crept through other years,
Shall cheer the seeker with their shining store.
Rude ridge of boulders, carn of polish'd crag!
Eternal utterer of the Deity,
I muse within thy shadow, and look up,

As on the face of the Invisible,
And sounds rush from thee in the tempest's clang,
And rattle round the portals of my soul,
Like oracles from the eternal hills;
And I have thought in childhood, when my feet
First press'd the mosses that hang down thy sides,
And bore me wondering 'mid thine isles of rock,
That on a night of tempest, wild and weird,
The Man i' the Moon had tumbled boulders down,
Which, rolling rudely, raised thee, root and rib.
I need no other monitor to show
The impress of Jehovah. Thou art full
Of the Eternal, and His voice is heard
Among the Druid temples of Carn Brea.

## *From* Destruction of the Cornish Tolmen

The coming years will miss it. Anxious eyes,
Stained deep with indignation, oft shall turn
To scan the site it dignified so long;
And the wild bird, the haunter of the hills,
Shall flounder in his passage, seeing not
His ancient landmark: whirling round and round
In strange bewilderment, with shriek and cry
He'll leave the heights for ever. Much I feel
To lose a boulder from my native moors,
As if a sister perished. Ye who love
The poetry of the mountains, guard, O guard
Our curious cromlechs! Let no hand of man
Destroy these stony prophets which the Lord
Has placed upon the tarns and sounding downs
With tones for distant ages.

# Fall of the Old Mine Stack

Man's noblest works will fall,
  The strongest arches crack,
And Earth's proudest cities all
  Be like the old mine stack.

At February's end,
  When clouds are often black.
In storm and pelting hail
  It fell, the old mine stack.

For long, long months it shook,
  As if upon the rack,
And then it toppled o'er
  At night, the old mine stack.

We watch'd it day by day,
  Smote with the storm-king black,
Till with a solemn roar
  Down dash'd the old mine stack.

The highest peak will fall,
  Earth's mighty zones will crack,
And Nature's bulwarks all
  Be like the old mine stack.


# *From* The Land's End

Yes, there are voices, echoes of the Past,
That rise from old Earth's silent solitudes,
And move along the crowded walks of men.
They flow among the roses of the spring,
On the stream's wavelets, in the wooing winds,
And mid the fresh drops of the vernal shower.
They ride upon the coursers of the storm,
Twang trumpet-like along the rocky ridge,
Wail round the ruins of the lonely shed,
And murmur by the cold forsaken hearth.
They float upon the billows of the deep,
Or howl among the breakers near to land:
They tremble in the flowing forest-odes,
And sing beneath the hamlet's spreading trees,
When morn is breaking, or the early Eve
Calls home the swallow 'neath her dusky robe;

Or when old Night is walking with the stars.
The earth is full of utterances sublime.

For me the rocks have language, and I've thought,
When gazing on those lichen'd chroniclers,
So stony-still, like giants clad in mail,
And slumbering on in awful dreaminess,
Of wondrous things that walk below the moon,
And feed on night-winds by the coppice-cave,
Or drink the dew from woven cups of moss,
Or dance upon the gilded heather-bells,
Or swing within the chalice of the flowers,
And glide around with golden imagery.
Nor gaze I on those hoary sentinels –
By field or fell, by castle or by cliff,
Lone in the waste, or by the village stream,
Or piled in dreadful heaps, crag over crag,
Like those around the wondrous Logan Rock,
Bare in the sunlight, dimly scann'd at eve,
Tissued with moonbeams, garnish'd with the stars,
Or frowning 'neath the sable weeds of night –
But tones of olden times come back again,
With dreams of song and visions of romance.

I walk'd the storm-swept, heather-hung Land's End,
And mused within its sea-wash'd galleries,
Whose granite arches mock the rage of Time.
I revell'd in the mystery of its shades,
And my soul soar'd up on the wings of song.
I treasured up the lore the sea-gulls taught,
Which in white clouds were cooing to the breeze.
I quaff'd the music of this granite grove,
And read rude cantos in the book of crags,
Stretching me in the theatre of heath,
When morn was breaking, and the light-house seem'd
An angel in the waters, and the rocks
Rang to the music of a thousand throats.
I look'd upon it as an awful poem,
Writ with the fingers of the Deity,
Whilst the proud billows of the mighty deep
Roll'd on their crests the awful name of God.

Who told thee that the scenes of other lands
Were far more beautiful than aught in mine?
Who told thee that the soothing sounds of song
Fell on the ear from classic fields afar
More musical than down our thymy braes?
Who told thee that the Alps and Appenines

Had more of wildness in their very names
Than all the wonders of our Cornish coast?
Ramble among our valleys, climb our hills,
Gaze on our bulwarks red at setting sun,
Mark well our bays strewn with the whitest sand,
Muse on our moors, and wonder in our mines;
Linger among our ivy-cover'd walls;
List the sweet breezes playing through the ferns,
Where sings the robin, and o'erhead the lark;
Stand by our castles and our monuments,
Our towns and hamlets and religious fanes;
And look upon the dark-green rocks that lie
Beneath the Atlantic surges, or on those
That tower on high in awful craggy peaks,
Rolling eternal diapasons wild
To the great billows' bass; and when within
The pillar'd grotto of the famed Land's End,
Bethink thee of the scenes of other shores,
And let thy heart be friendly to mine own.

Oft in my sleep I've trod the land of dreams,
And worshipp'd mid its still sublimity.
I've climb'd the back of some dark jagged cloud,
Rolling through chaos; and methought I've heard
The breathing spirit of infinity.
I've wandered by clear streamlets far away,
Which seem'd more musical than aught of earth;
I've travell'd valleys starr'd with radiant flowers,
And wept upon my silent harp for joy;
I've scaled black mountains where the huge rocks rose
In grim array, a ghostly multitude,
Lifting their rough heads to the icy moon,
And shivering there in silent majesty;
And I have walk'd among them joyously,
Feasting my spirit on their vision'd forms,
And then, awaking, wonder'd 'twas a dream.
But when I found me on the rough Land's End,
Conning the numbers which the winds and waves
Had channell'd on its pillars, not a dream
But seem'd outrivall'd by this craggy host.

Time plucks the coronet from kingly brows,
And scathes the laurel in the wreath of fame;
The glory of man's greatest work departs,
And o'er it drops the drapery of decay.
The hero, and the hero's blazon'd deeds,
Though carved in marble, drizzled o'er with blood,
From memory fade, and shrink into the dark.

The fancy-palace built up by the bard
With its own echoes breaks and disappears;
But those eternal everlasting rocks
Sing the same cadence to the solemn sea,
And stand up strangely in their bright shell-cloaks,
With their great Maker's name upon their tongues,
As when the Pilgrim Fathers' misty eyes
Beheld them fade forever from their view.


## *From* Kynance Cove[18]

I've been to fairy-land, and seen the fays
Unvested in their workshop. Scenes were here
That held a poet captive with their charms,
And mock'd his fancy like a thing of gloom.
The wondrous cliffs were polish'd with the waves,
And flash'd and flicker'd like huge mineral walls.
Their scaly sides were clothed with leafy gold,
And burn'd with beauty in the light of day.
The sands that lay on this Elysian cove
Were all ring-straked with painted serpentine.
The hollow caves the waves had fretted out
Were dashed with images of flowery hues;
And on the rocks, like beautiful psalm-leaves,
Were odes of music lovely as the light,
Trill'd by the sea nymphs in their watery robes.

I'm fond of travelling old deserted paths,
Search'd with the winds and soft with solitude;
I'm fond of grandeur in its robe of crags,
Or fringed with flowers, or edged with velvet moss;
Of grand old forests, where the trees stand up
And shout together, "God hath made us all!" –
Of odorous heaths, that oft inspire my Muse,
And lift me high on Inspiration's steep;
Of musing lonely by old Ocean's shore,
And roaming wildly through the fields of thought;
While castles, towers, and palaces uprise,
Built with chaste light, and roof'd with burning gems.
But starting from my song-trance one bright morn,
And turning down yon crooked heather-lane,
These fancy pictures floated in the dark,
As rock on rock uncurtain'd to my gaze,
And roll'd upon my vision like a spell.

Hail, fairy-featured, beautiful Kynance!
A loving smile is ever on thy face,
And Beauty revels mid thy gold arcades.
Along thy glittering grottoes tones are heard
Like songs at evening by some distant lake.
Thy colour'd crags, on which the sea-birds perch,
Are tuneful with the tread of tiny feet.
No harsh discordant sound is heard in thee;
And he who journeys through these sculptured creeks,
And gazes on those hills of serpentine,
Where Nature sits upon her chisell'd throne,
Smiling benignly in her samphire robes,
Wearing her best, her craggy crown of gems,
When cluster'd once more in his loving home,
Will feel a sweetness flowing through his heart,
And more exalted views of Nature's God.

Why seek for beauty in the stranger's clime,
When Beauty's state-room is the gay Kynance?
Why seek for visions courted by the Muse?
When Kynance opens like a mine of gems?
Why seek for language from the waves' white lips
When ocean fills this pictured Cove with hymns?
Why seek for caverns striped with natural lays,
When they are gouged here by the surging sea?
Why seek for islands girdled with the main,
When Kynance holds them in her feathery folds?
So mused I in the sea-damp Drawing-Room,
While through the Bellows rush'd a flood of song.

# My Infant Daughter Falling Asleep On My Knee

How softly dost thou fall asleep,
  Sweet cherub, on my knee!
No bird can sing itself to rest
  More carelessly than thee.

There's not a thought-stain on thy cheek,
  No sorrow in thine eye;
Thou lookest like the wing of peace,
  As thou asleep dost lie.

Five minutes since I heard thy song,
  And stroked thy little head;

But now I lay thee down to rest
  Within thy cradle-bed.

And once, my mother tells me now,
  I fell asleep like thee,
Without a care-mark on my brow,
  Upon my father's knee.

Sleep on, sleep on, my innocent!
  When years are sped away,
O may thy rest be then as sweet
  As it is now this day!
And when at last I fall asleep
  In death, O, let it be
As calm and quiet as my babe's,
  When slumbering on my knee.


## On Treslothan Chapel[19]

Peal on, ye gentle preachers. Day is done,
And eve steals down the vale in garments grey:
I ponder in her shadows. One sweet spot
Is ever with me, as your echoes float
Above the tree-tops, like the sweep of wings.
A little grave it is among the hills,
Beside a Gothic chapel, and I seem
To hear the tread of those who haste to prayer,
Through primrose lanes, although I'm far away.
Here have I long desired to sleep at last,
When life, with all its cares, is at an end,
Among the honest, pious villagers,
Just at the foot of my old granite mount;
That when the cottager, his day's work done,
Sits in the dusk with baby on his knee,
What time the first few tapers gild the pane,
He, listening to the river at his gate,
May think of him who caroll'd through his moors.


## *From* Camborne

Time chisels out the foot-prints of the Past,
Planing away old hieroglyphic scars,
Gashing strange notches in his calendar,

And raising, on the ashes of an hour,
New wonders, to be wondrous and decay.

How like a thing of magic hast thou rose
Out of the copper-caverns of the earth,
Graceful and plain, poetically neat, –
The cottage, homes of those that work below,
Where sun, or star, or silver-margin'd cloud,
Or tree, or flower, or bird, or murmuring brook,
Or chiming breeze, or tuneful waterfall,
Is never seen or heard! How like a thing
That leap'd into existence at a nod,
Art thou, my native Camborne! girded round
With mead, and meadow-land and shady grove,
And boundary-lines of sweetest earthly bliss!

.................................................................

I came, – was lead along thy narrow streets,
Stood in thy porches, heard the hum of those
Who long have slept beneath the grassy sod,
Gazed at thy toy-shop windows, – gazed and gazed,
Until I thought the little horses moved,
And snapp'd their bitless bridles! then again
Rubb'd both mine eyes to see the gingerbread,
Like gilded soldiers, marching on the stall,
With lions, tigers, bears, and elephants,
And images of beasts before the Flood,
Grotesque and strange, wild, knotty, limbless things;
So that I leap'd and clapp'd my hands for joy;
And, when I sat again on mother's knee,
I thought that I had realised my dream,
Had seen the very centre of the world,
And knew all bright and precious things were there,
And told her stories three or four months long.

.................................................................

Thou hast thy solemn grave-yard, and thy tombs,
Where like the ashes of our pilgrim-sires,
Grass cover'd graves, and some without a blade,
Trees weeping dew-drops at the vesper-time,
And flowers that tell us all is calm below.
Here rich and poor are "huddled out of sight,"
And sweetly sleep together; not a sigh
Disturbs the halcyon of their dreamless rest!
Without its pale, a thousand voices roar
And hiss unmeaning torture! but, within,
A solemn silence sits on every bough,
And creeps with silken feet along the grass;

Voices, unseen, are whispering to the soul;
And in the tower are heard the feet of Death.

.............................................

It is for this I love thee; for I've thought,
Ay, often thought, that my last sleep should be
In the still churchyard of my native town!
Here lie my sire and grandsire, side by side;
And here a little sister, a span long;
And I have thought, – but no, it must not be;
O let me moulder where my daughter sleeps!
That I would hang my wild harp o'er my tomb,
And go to sleep beside them! – Fare thee well!
The silver moon unveils her lovely face,
And gazes down upon thy twilight bowers,
As if she really loved thee! flinging floods
Of silver pencilling across thy robes,
And bathing thee in beauty! O, 'tis sweet
Here in the moonlight to look down and see
The moonbeams dancing on thy cottage-roofs!
It will be even so when we are gone,
And sleeping in our graves. – Once more, farewell!

# The Emigrant's Departure

He stood upon his native mount,
    And gazed upon the sky:
'Twas bluer than 'twas wont to be,
    Or *look'd* so to his eye.
And when the evening sun went down
    Behind the wavy west,
The tear-drop glisten'd in his eye,
    And heaved his labouring breast.

The music of the evening bells
    Came on the harping breeze;
And O how sweet, how passing sweet,
    It floated through the trees!
Dame Nature tuned her sweetest lyre,
    Or *seem'd* to tune it, then:
He never heard such melody,
    Nor hoped to hear again!

The peasants in the vale below
    Were at their evening meal;

And when the merry village hum
  Did o'er his senses steal,
He turned away his aching eye
  From scenes so dear beneath,
And dropp'd a tear in solitude
  Upon the rustling heath.

O! there were notes too sweet to last,
  That swept across the plain;
And there were shadows of the past,
  That flash'd athwart his brain:
And there were in his watery eye,
  Around him and above,
In every corner of the sky,
  Sweet images of love!

He thought the first bright flowers of May
  Had never look'd so fair,
As when his last long lingering glance
  He bent upon them there.
He kiss'd the little murmuring stream
  Within his native dell,
And, as the evening star came forth,
  He sigh'd his last farewell!

The moon arose, and shower'd her beams
  Upon the ivied rocks,
And twined her silver tissues with
  The mountain's heather-locks;
When, with his hawthorn staff in hand,
  He left his cottage-door,
And wander'd to a foreign land,
  To see his home no more.


## *From* Luda: A Lay of the Druids

The furze and heather are in bloom,
The moors are fragrant with perfume;
Afar is heard the hum of bees,
Whose murmurs mingle with the trees.
The waters flow the fens among,
The skylark fills the glades with song,
And in the wood where Summer strays
The throstle like a poet plays.
O now to tread some hillock high,
To catch the breeze that murmurs by

From banks of thyme and beds of flowers,
Where Nature rears her own green bowers,
And tunes her harp, and sings for aye
Her soothing everlasting lay!
My Cornwall! what a land is thine
For crag and cross, for moor and mine!
Thy hills are zoned with copper ore;
Thy vales yield tin, a precious store;
The greenest grass thy glades afford;
Thy sheltered bays with fish are stored;
Thy granite carns are castle-crowned,
Where altar-heaps and forts are found.
No brooks are clearer than thine own,
Which steal by cave and cromlech stone;
And every hill-top in the land
Is marked by rude tradition's hand.
Sweet wild-flowers hang their lamps of love
By path below and rift above.
Thy sons are brave, thy daughters fair,
And none can with thy wives compare.

The sun was shining on the lake,
When the good palmer sought the brake.
Leaving the castle on the right,
He walked along the ledgy height
Towards an opening in the wood,
Where a rough Druid temple stood.
For well he knew by sight and sound,
From distant vale and rising ground,
And cottage nestled by the mere,
That a religious rite was near:
And hence he travelled on and strove
Before mid-day to reach the grove
Beyond the rude gorseddau-seat,[20]
Where the wild worshippers would meet.

Adown the glen on palfrey white
And aged Druid comes in sight:
His long beard on his breast is spread,
And oaken leaves adorn his head;
A sash does round his body meet,
And shoes of wood are on his feet;
His snowy garments reach his heels,
Which the light prancing palfrey feels;
And figures on his vest appear,
A serpent's head and crescent clear.
Six different badges mark his store;
The King could only wear one more.

The horse-rein doth his right hand hold,
His left uplifts a hook of gold;[21]
And as he climbs the sacred mound,
His eyes are fixed upon the ground.
Behind him comes a motley throng,

Thus chanting as they walk along:
"The crescent moon, the crescent moon,
In six days old this pleasant noon:
Again the new year is at hand,
Green leaves and flowerets fill the land.
So to the silent grove we go
To cut the golden mistletoe."


## Wearing Out

Wearing out! wearing out!
Yes, dear wife, we're wearing out.
The clock-fly points to ten, or more,
And some one knocketh at the door.
Wearing out, wearing out.

Wearing out! wearing out!
Yes, dear wife, we're wearing out.
Let the life-beat house-walls shake,
We will not complain, or quake.
Wearing out, wearing out.

Wearing out! wearing out!
Yes, dear wife, we're wearing out.
But the love vouchsafed of yore
Shall attend us evermore.
Wearing out, wearing out.

Wearing out! wearing out!
Yes, dear wife, we're wearing out.
And another land is near,
Where old age will disappear.
Wearing out, wearing out.

## Margaret Ann Courtney 1834–1920

## A Picture

A coming tide, a stretch of gray, wet sand,
A sunset sky, with gold and crimson bright,
Across the sea a rippling path of light.
Weed-covered stones, hollows where clear pools stand,
A crazy boat left lying on the strand.
Low rounded hills that to the sea slope down,
A straggling, whitewashed, little fishing town,
Thin mists of evening creeping o'er the land.
A ridge of wind-blown trees against the sky,
Two women home returning wearily
From mussel-picking; wet with sea and spray,
Bare-legged, with creel on back plodding their way.
Men gazing seaward, leaning on a wall,
Sweet summer twilight brooding over all.


## The White Ladie

Now, fifty years ago, may be,
  On a wild winter's night,
To the ceaseless moaning of the sea,
This legend of the "White Ladie"
  Was told by firelight.

She was a proud and haughty dame
  Of old Penkivell's race;
He had no son to bear his name;
He worshipped her, and who could blame,
  In the old Squire's place?

Though centuries have passed away,
  Her home may still be seen, –
A granite building, low and grey,
Storm-beaten, often flecked with spray,
  In the parish of Pendeen.

Her name was Avis; there were few
  In Cornwall fair as she,
Her eyes were a deep hyacinth blue,
Her cheeks had the pink creamy hue
  We in the wild rose see.

Her hair was red, with gleams of gold,
　And rippled round her head;
But she was false, – her heart was cold;
Her soul for money she'd have sold;
　Pride was her daily bread.

From all the parishes around
　Brave suitors came to woo;
But in her sight none favour found,
She cared more for her horse and hound
　Than loyal hearts and true.

Would only no denial take
　Her uncle Uther's son;
He thought of her asleep, awake;
He courted dangers for her sake,
　And vowed she should be won.

For her he'd often crossed the sea
　In search of laces rare,
Brocades and silks, that she might be
Decked out in all her bravery,
　The fairest of the fair.

For Cornishmen, in days of yore,
　Thought smuggling was no crime;
And John Lenine, who knew the shore,
Had brought from France, like many more,
　Rich ventures in his time.

A secret subterranean way
　Ran 'twixt her house and beach;
Through a dark cave the entrance lay,
Known to few dwellers in the bay, –
　Most difficult to reach.

But dangers never daunted John;
　By it one night he brought
Avis, when folks to rest had gone,
Some gauds she'd set her heart upon;
　To win her thus he thought.

She took his gifts, but mocked his woe:
　Said, "Cousin, this I'll do,
When summer comes with frost and snow,
Or roses in mid-winter blow,
　Why then – I'll marry you!"

"I swear I will. Next Christmas-day
  A red rose to me bring,
My answer then shall not be nay,
And as a pledge for what I say,
  You may – give me a ring."

In a few days the ring was sent,
  And then John sail'd afar;
In quest of the red rose he went;
To wed her still his soul was bent;
  Hope was his guiding star.

He had been gone three months or more;
  Christmas was drawing nigh;
Slipped in, and anchored close to shore,
A man-of-war, that once before,
  In Pendeen Bay did lie.

Of her were many stories told, –
  How, under shade of night,
She'd sent forth men, like wolves on fold,
Who'd carried off the young and old,
  For James, the King, to fight.

This dreadful ship returned again,
  Made many women sad:
Some feared to lose their boys: with pain
Some wept for husbands "pressed" and slain;
  Avis alone was glad.

She knew the captain, – thought that he
  Could wealth and rank bestow;
For them he might her husband be,
For never wed a man would she
  Who could no rent-roll show.

He was not there to woo a bride,
  For men alone he came;
But still he flattered, fed her pride,
With honeyed words and gifts he plied
  This most imperious dame.

Because through her he wished to learn
  The secret hidden way,
From whence it ran, where made a turn,
When John was likely to return,
  And why he'd gone away?

The traitress told him all – The vow
    She'd pledged herself to keep;
Said John at home would soon be now;
Wished he would "press him," cared not how;
    If killed, she should not weep.

Meanwhile poor John, who'd sailed away,
    The bright, red rose to find,
Had heard in Nice a sailor say
"That roses bloomed on Christmas-day,"
    And Fate to him was kind.

For, walking down a crooked street,
    There in a house he spied
A rose-tree bearing blossoms sweet;
He entered in with eager feet,
    Nor long did there abide

Before 'twas his. Full many a crown
    For that rose-bush he paid.
Quick to his ship he bore it down,
Again set sail for Penzance town,
    And a prosperous voyage made.

His tree he guarded with great care,
    But the flowers faded fast;
Its branches soon were nearly bare
Of all its blossoms late so fair, –
    One rose remained – the last.

He reached his home on Christmas-day
    As the joy-bells out did ring;
Red rose in hand, he went his way
To meet his cousin, blithe and gay;
    His heart did carols sing.

He bent his steps towards the shore
    The hidden path to take,
But ere he reached the secret door,
Set on him ten stout men or more,
    A captive him to make.

He fought for life, whilst holding still
    The red rose in his hand;
And many of his foes did kill, –
Was wounded oft, yet fought on, till
    Lay stretched upon the sand

He and the Captain side by side,
  Both bleeding unto death.
The treachery of his would-be bride
John heard, – spake not a word, and died;
  But with his dying breath

The Captain cursed her; bade a lad
  The rose to Avis bear,
Wet with his blood: "Tell her she had
Her wicked wish, might now be glad,
  And it in triumph wear."

She lived till she was very old,
  But never from that day
The sun shone on her; she was cold
In hottest June, for she had sold
  And sworn a life away.

No shadow from her body cast
  E'er played upon the ground.
Shunned by all men, she lived alone,
And when death claimed her for his own,
  Her soul no respite found.

Each Christmas morn she doth appear,
  At the entrance o' the cave,
Holding her rose. She striketh fear:
Who sees her knows the coming year
  Will find him in his grave.

Jas Roberts 1838–c.1910

# A Dirge on Maen Rock[1]

Tolmen! thy glory's gone,
Thy grandeur is no more,
No longer dost thou stand
Majestic as of yore.

On that exalted crest,
Thy head was raised on high,
The winters' storms and blasts
Thou proudly did defy.

Through countless centuries
Unsolved the mystery:
No speech nor language e'er
Made known thy history.

Dumb the geologist,
The antiquarian,
Thy swan song may I sing
*Octogenarian*?

On to thy dizzy top
With ladder did I climb
And wonderlingly beheld
The hollows scooped by Time,

Defiant didst thou stand
With thy expanded chest;
From far couldst thou be seen,
The Pride of Cornwall West.

On two small granite rocks
Fantastically perched;
'Tween these I stood beneath,
In vain thy secret searched.

'Twixt these sustaining rocks
On did I clamber through,
Thy giant weight above,
Yet none had I to rue.

When weird Tregeagle[2] stalked the land
Throughout the West Countrie,
From Tintagel to Lizard Point,
Was his shade known to thee?

When fairies danced at Merry Meet
In ancient Constantine,
From Pixies' Hall turned they their feet
As to foregather round thy seat,
Or worship at thy shrine?

In times when *Centauri* held sway,
Thou monarch of them all;
But no perfidious Nestor thou,
No Hercules wrought thy fall.

Down through uncounted aeons
Unchanged was thy sway;
Did poet e'er invoke the Muse
Thy wonders to portray?

But men of nineteenth century born,
Cast longing eyes on thee;
Six hundred tons of granite stone,
Good value did they see.

Then to himself said he who held
Of mineral rights the fee:
"These granite rocks are worth a whole
King's ransom now to me."

No doubt that for a certain sum
These rights he would forego;
Now Cornishmen these terms will ye
Accept? Say "Yes" or "No."

Hear Constantine and Falmouth too,
Heed Helston and Penryn:
On these conditions would he cede
His interest therein.

Alas! from Truro to Penzance
Comes no responsive word;
The doom of Tolmen soon was sealed,
Faint protest was there heard,

Alas! all sentiment,
All hail material gain!
We count thy worth in good hard cash,
We nineteenth century men.

Antiquity and mystery,
Mythology and history,

The halo that encircled thee,
The reverence that was due to thee,
All ruthlessly ignored.
Down deep into the quarry rolled,
By jumper, borer, wert thou holed,
That thou for *profit* might be sold,
Thus mercilessly bored.

From all thy majesty down driven,
By sledge, and ripper, feather riven,
Thus blotted out from under heaven!

From thy proud pedestal o'erthrown,
By pack, and mallet, chisel, hewn,
Shaped into many blocks of stone!

Then borne to other lands and climes,
A sacrifice to dollars, dimes,
Of these materialistic times!

Some humble place thy fragments fill
In distant lands or near;
But where they are, and what they do,
And what their final destiny too,
There's no one seems to care.

Cornubia! Cornubia!
Thy stupor we bewail;
In visions of the future thou
Didst miserably fail.

Tolmen! in glorious was thy fall
From thy sublime estate:
But while life's lamp holds out to burn,
Where'er I go, where'er I turn,
One son of Constantine will mourn
Thy ignominious fate.

**Joseph Thomas 1840–1894**

## Kitty Cornish

Come all ye jolly tinners, who
  To Camborne Town belong,
Sit down and touch your pipe, my dears,
  And listen to my song;
Hundreds of fitty-looking maids
  In Camborne you may see,
But little Kitty Cornish is
  The crop of the bunch to me.

I saw her as I came from Bal,
  Her gook,[1] I caan't tell how,
Fell back upon her nuddick,[2] and
  The sun shone on her brow;
Her cruddy hair was plethoned up
  So beautiful to see,
And little Kitty Cornish is
  The crop of the bunch to me.

Her smile was bright as May, her cheeks
  Had caught the rose's hue,
Her eyes were blue as guckoo flowers,
  And sparkled like the dew.
Her lips were red as haggalans[3]
  Full ripe upon the tree;
And little Kitty Cornish is
  The crop of the bunch to me.

I called – she had her towser[4] on,
  A mooling[5] of the bread;
And as she put the dough to plum,
  This here is what I said:
'I'd like some of that fuggan,[6] dear,
  If I may stay to tea.'
And little Kitty Cornish is
  The crop of the bunch to me.

I've heard the lark sing in the sky,
  The grey bird in the brake,
I've heard the choir at 'Wesley,'
  (That's grand, and no mistake);
But sweeter far her whisper, when
  She promised for to be
My own dear Kitty Cornish, and
  The crop of the bunch to me.

'Tis sweet to feel the sunshine, as
  You come from underground;
'Tis sweet to breathe the fresh, fresh air,
  And see the flowers around;
But sweeter than the sunlight,
  Or honey from the bee,
Is my own dear Kitty Cornish –
  The crop of the bunch to me.

**Mark Guy Pearse 1842–1930**

# Cornwall

Thou hardy Mother of a hardy race,
Cornwall, thy hosts of songs are proud of thee;
Scattered abroad in many a distant place,
Our deep, our stedfast love is true to thee.

We count no skies so fair as those at home;
No cliffs like those that guard the Western shore;
We see again the tossing billows foam,
We see the golden furze about the moor.

We know the valleys sloping to the sea;
The wooded sides about the winding stream;
The dripping mill-wheel with its greenery;
Wet sands aglow with crimson sunset gleam.

As doth the eagle, when her young can fly,
Break up the nest that they may know their power,
And learn to soar into the utmost sky,
And sweep defiant of the storm and shower,

So dost thou seek to make thy children brave:
The engine-house is silent on the hill;
The rubbish heaps are grass-grown as the grave;
The kibble thrown aside, the chains are still;

And now wherever hide the veins of ore,
There toil thy sons with brain and skilful hands;
From Spain and Africa to Chili's shore
They give the world the wealth of far-off lands.

The lonely dweller 'mid the city's host,
Where no man greets his brother in the way,
Thrills with new life in vision of the coast
Where the wild billows break in showers of spray.

Amid the hard and grasping ways of life
Comes a sweet breath as of some better clime,
A holy spell that calms the fevered strife,
In thought of those who fill that happier time.

Though scattered wide throughout the busy earth,
No matter where the Cornishman may be,
We love and bless the country of our birth;
Our Mother, One and All are proud of Thee.

# The Miner in Foreign Parts: California

"Aw my dear life! well, iss, of course,
  'Tis very fine, you're right, –
A hundred miles and more of plains,
  And then the mountains' height;
The valley and the waterfall,
  Beside the towering tree.
But bless 'ee, 'tisn't nothin', sir,
  To which I can see."

"A stretch of furze bush all ablaze,
  Another stretch of fern;
A patch of purple heather bloom,
  And then you take a turn;
You pass great piles of rubbish heaps,
  You pass a bal that's knacked;[1]
And then a whitewashed cottage peeps
  From where the corn is stacked."

"I see the garden through the gate,
  I hear the hum of bees,
The butterflies are everywhere,
  The birds sing in the trees.
The flowers – that's the sort I love,
  Sweet Williams pink and red,
The boy's-love grows beside the door;
  The jessamine's overhead;"

"The fuchsia blooms most all the year,
  The happy roses creep
About the window of the place,
  Where my dear maid do sleep;
To think they greet her at the dawn,
  To think that their sweet bloom
Should breathe about my awn, my awn,
  And fill that little room!"

"I see her standing at the gate
  When milking time is done;
And all the sea and sky is red
  With setting of the sun;
The golden glory of it all
  Is shining in her hair.
The flowers at her bosom
  Are not more sweet or fair."

"Aw, my dear life, I tell 'ee what,
  When I do think of she
Your gold is but a little thing –
  The only gold for me
Is just enough to make a ring,
  To tell the world she's mine
And diamonds – I'd rather see
  Her blessed eyes ashine."

"The glory of your scenery
  Sinks all into the shade
Beside the thought of her I love,
  My awn sweet little maid.
How poor a thing it seems to me
  To be a millionaire,
Beside a kiss from those dear lips,
  My little maid so fair!"

## The Miner in Foreign Parts: Australia

"Zacky,[2] my boy, come here and sit down,
  Lev us touch pipe for a bit;
The heat is enough to kill a chap
  Down there in the stifflin' pit;
Come under the shade of the big gum-tree –
  'Tis a purty place for to sit."

"Had any news from home, have 'ee, then?
  A paper you used to receive."
And Zacky was still for a brave long time,
  Then he gave a sigh and a heave:
"I ha'n't heard now for ever so long,
  But 'tis my fault, I believe."

"You see, I been goin' from place to place,
  And 'twas hard to find time to write,
And when you've been working all day long,
  You're 'most too tired at night."
And Zacky was still again for a while –
  "Here, comrade, give me a light."

"And so they didn't know where to send,
  It must be three months or so;
But let me see – why, 'tis more than that,

Well, how quick the time do go!
'Tis nearer six months since I wrote home;
  The post's so far off, you know."

"But I wrote to mother yesterday" –
  And Zacky wiped off a tear,
"And I sent her a present, a lumpin' sum
  That will keep her half a year;
I know it will make her old heart sing –
  God bless her, I wish she was here."

"'Twas a dream I had – 'twill do 'ee good
  For to hear what I've got to say –
For all I do feel a bit ashamed,
  I'm feelin' better today;
And you know, comrade, how easy it is
  To forget when folks is away."

"Well, you mind the little place at home, –
  There's just a bit of a lane
Going down from the road, the left-hand side, –
  I could see it all so plain.
And mother, she stood in the cottage door,
  And her face was full of pain."

"The garden was all in sun and shade,
  'Twas such a beautiful day;
The lark sung up in the blue, blue sky;
  I could smell the scent of the hay;
And the postman was comin' down the lane,
  A hurryin' on his way."

"And mother, she lifted up her face,
  And waited till he come near;
But he went on. 'There's nothing for you.
  I'm sorry, Mrs Tregeare,'
For he saw the grief that filled her eyes –
  God bless 'ee, mother dear."

"And then she went into the little room,
  And she stood by the fireplace –
Her hair's turned grey, and the lines gone deep
  Since last I saw that face.
And then she lifted her hand and took
  A photograph out of a case."

"'Twas a thing that I sent her years ago,
  And she brought it into the light;

She looked at it with a bitten lip,
  And I saw that her face was white,
And she sighed as she kissed it tenderly,
  *I wonder if he's all right!"*
"So I wrote to mother yesterday,"
  And Zacky wiped off a tear,
"And sent her a present, a lumpin' sum,
  That will keep her half a year,
And I'm going to write her again next mail –
  God bless 'ee, mother dear!"


# The Fisherman's Song

I'm sittin' in my li'll boat;
  The lines is to the stern;
And all my thoughts are full of 'ee
  Whichever way I turn.

If you was this here li'll boat
  And I was but the sea,
Aw, my dear life, I tell 'ee, though,
  It should be fine for thee.

My curling waves around the keel
  Should dance with happy light;
I'd bear 'ee past the sunken rocks
  And bring 'ee home all right.

If you was this here li'll boat
  And I was but the sky,
Aw, dear, what sunshine you should have –
  The day should never die.

I'd bring 'ee such a gentle breeze
  And fill the pretty sail;
Whichever way you want to go
  The wind should never fail.

If you was this here li'll boat
  And I was but the sea,
Aw, dear, what lovely fish and things
  I'd bring to gladden 'ee.

What crabs and lobsters you should have
  What lovely conger eels,

And now and then a salmon bass,
  And then some salmon peels.

I'd send 'ee up a halibut;
  The biggest of the prawn;
And 'pon your birthday you should have
  A pet whale for you awn.

I'd make the mackerel jump aboard,
  The pilchard and the hake,
The cod and great big flying fish
  Should come up for your sake.

And scores of pretty mermaidens,
  A-combin' of their hair,
Should bring 'ee gifts of pearl and shells
  To deck 'ee all so fair.

I'm sittin' in my li'll boat;
  The gulls is in the sky;
Aw, dear, if I was one of they,
  I knaw which way I'd fly.


# The Hopeless Dawn[3]

'Twas a Friday in August, the last of the month,
  With a sunset so pretty as ever could be,
And a breeze just enough for to fill out the sails –
  *Can 'ee hear the raven a-croak in the tree?*

My man and my son had a craft of their own –
  The Beauty they called her, so proud of the name,
She was called after mother, so both of them said –
  *The wind is gone west and the sky is a flame!*

My son he was wed, and he brought home his bride;
  For father and me loved the maid as our own
So sweet as her looks and so clever as good –
  *There's the cry of the gulls and the sea is a moan!*

I had dreamed for three nights of a terrible storm,
  And thought I stood out in the teeth of the gale,
And I woke with my watching in vain for the craft –
  *Can 'ee hear the waves break with a sob and a wail?*

We went to the door for to look at the stars,
  As she and me did before going up to bed;
They was all of a tremble as if in a fright –
  *That's a rocket they've fired 'pon Black Rock head!*

Then all of a sudden came the burst of the storm;
  Like thunder there broke the roar of the swell;
And the wind seemed to shake the house and the ground –
  *Can 'ee hear it, my dear – the toll of the bell?*

I sat down on the chair, and she lay on the floor,
  And she sobbed as she laid her head on my knee
We waited and prayed – but twas waiting in vain –
  *There's the boom of a gun from a ship out at sea!*

The fire was dead and the candle burnt out;
  Day broke with a sea and a sky that was grey;
But for us two the sun has not risen since then –
  *A wreck on the point, did the fishermen say?*

**Katharine Lee Jenner 1854–1936**

## O Mystic Land

O mystic Land, what sign
   From things that are divine
Passes from thee and thine
   To us who are between
These mysteries, whose veil
Half drawn reveals how frail
   The texture of the web 'twixt seen and things unseen?

The light that falls on thee
   Is coloured diversely
With rainbow hues, which flee
   Ere we can note their tint.
Here nothing lingers long,
But passes as a song,
   Whose melody is echo ere we catch its hint.

On thee a glamour lies,
   Inconstant as thy skies,
Whose shadow, falling, hies
   Quickly as it doth fall,
As changeful as the tides,
Whose heaving shows and hides
   Thy patient feet of rock set in their briny pall.

Those hoary stones of old
   Which crown thy hills and hold
Life's secrets in their fold,
   Thou guardest sacredly.
None knows what worship rude,
Whose martyr blood imbrued
   Those silent altar stones, which now lie nakedly.

On every vale and hill
   Are holy names, which still
Can stir men's hearts and thrill
   With love of holy deeds,
By Saints and Martyrs done,
Who won their deathless crown
   For sowing in thy soil the blessed Gospel seeds.

O Land of mist and song,
   Wild waters set among,
In thy sons' hearts there throng
   Thy heartsick melodies.

They catch the echoes faint
Of thy long wail and plaint,
   The voices of the past which are thy symphonies.


# The Old Names

The half-forgotten music of old names
   Clings to the rocks and hills,
And an intangible human fragrance gives
   To senseless earth, and fills
With glamour half divine all the wild places,
   Recalling the old days,
When man on earth believed that the Divine
   Encompassed all his ways.

Out of the vast void of oblivion
   Rings the wild melody
Of those old words, whose only resting-place
   Is the vague memory
Of man, the creature so prone to forget,
   Yet who forgetting clings,
Subconsciously remembering their sense,
   To the old names and things.

The music of the old names is worn thin
   By busy lips of men;
Yet they are eloquent of ancient dreams
   Of knightly valour, when
The hills were purpled and the valleys stained
   With battles and sore strife,
And of the deeds, achievements, hope and fears,
   Of long-forgotten life.

Come to Carn Brea, beside Trevorian Down,
   And hear the Gwynver[1] call
From Vellandreath, Carn Bargas, and Carn Ky,
   While evening shadows fall
On Tregonebris and Boscawen-Oon,
   And over Crows-an-Wra
And on Bartinny and Caer Brane there shines
   The light of dying day.

Away beyond Rospannel and Boscarn,
   And Buryan tower above,
The southern sea is gleaming through the gap,
   That marks Lamorna Cove,

And all about St Levan and Penberth
   On to Pedn-Men-an-Mere
The sunset shines upon a land whose names
   Are music everywhere.

These names of our dead speech are music still
   In our dear living land,
Which never can be void or desolate
   While here on every hand
Is still the record of our father's lives,
   Though their old hopes and fears
Have passed away like sunlight on the hills
   Down through the path of years.

## Can Gwlasol, Agan Mam-Vro / Anglice, a Patriotic Song for our Motherland

Throned above the western sea,
   Battleground of forces grim,
Holy motherland, for thee
   We thy children raise our hymn;
Scattered over all the earth
   Loving hearts we turn alway
To the Land that gave us birth,
   And for thee our voices pray.

On the billows wild and free,
   In the darkness of the mine,
Wheresoe'er thy children be
   Evermore they shall be thine;
Thine in thoughts of sounding seas,
   Downs with heath and furze aglow,
Thine in glorious memories
   Of thy heroes long ago.

Thine was Arthur, thine his knights,
   Strong Geraint, his admiral,
Lancelot of a hundred fights,
   Tristan, Gawain, Percival.
Thine were they in shining mail
   Through thy forest ways who trod,
Seeking for the Holy Grail,
   Mystery of the Faith of God.

To that Faith thy sons were true,
        In its hour of darkest night,
Dared to die, a faithful few,
        Worsted in that hopeless fight.
Sons of thine with Grenville fell
        For their King in Lansdown's fray;
Let the Royal Letter tell
        How they failed him not that day.

Michael of the Guarded Mount,
        Saints before God's Face who stand,
Keyna of the hallowed fount,
        Piran of the drifting sand,
Petrock of the iron shore,
        Ruan of the southern strand,
Ia, Breage – a hundred more,
        Watch and ward our native land!
One and all, on you we call;
        Pray for Cornwall, One and All![2]

# On the Cliff

We are lying here in the glamour of the grey
By the ineffable dim sweetness of the sea.
All glaring sunlight is tempered by the spray,
Spun of their dews in the salt sweetness of the air,
Thus tuned to our sad souls set in sin's array,
Holding all colour yet sicklied over with shade.
For the Saints is the golden glory of the day;
For the dead is the deep black velvet of the night;
For us set in between, the glitter of the grey.

# O Lone Grey Land

O lone grey land, the wild wind whispers thee
  Of all things sweet and soft, tender and true.
Round thee the circling murmurs of the sea
  Compass thy shores with web of living blue,
  Blending in one in faint, sweet harmony
  Their living voices o'er the long dead past.
O sweet grey land, wilt thou speak clear at last?
        O lone grey land.

O sad grey land, whom russet ferns make brown
  Between the golden pyre of yellow blooms,
And purple bells of heather thickly strown,
  You hold your secrets hid in rocky tombs
  Or mystic circles on bare moors alone.
  How many broken hearts, great vanished dreams
Lie under your grey stones, beside your streams,
        O lone grey land!


## On the Coast (Cornish Fisher-Girl's Lament)

      Gold the corn within the shock,
        Blue the water o'er the rock,
      Blood red poppies on the land,
        Brown the sea weed on the strand; –
Oh my lost love, Oh my dear Love, who sailed away,
Of what avail to me that there be sun to-day?

      Peep the mountain o'er the fields,
        Watching what the water yields;
      Sail the boats out of the wrack,
        As sailed those which ne'er came back;
Oh my lost love, Oh my dear Love, with my youth gone past,
Is there a gleaming shore where we may meet at last?

      Purple moors upon the hills,
        To the sea flow down the rills,
      Rain the clouds upon its breast; –
        Give to those who lie there rest.
Oh my lost love, Oh my dear Love, break the day for me,
When we two may stand beside the eternal sea.


## A Grey Day

Pale glory of the grey,
  When sea and sky afar
  Together blended are,
The sun lets not one ray
  Escape from out the folds
  Of tender grey which holds
Earth, sea and sky in grey.

A faint translucent haze
   Floats over water wan,
   And baffles eyes which scan
The waves, where on fair days
   The world and sky would meet
   And form a mercy seat
To hold the sun's last rays.

The grey creeps into me;
   To-day there is no sun;
   Earth, sea, and sky are one.
Thy dead lie still in thee,
   Perhaps to-day, to-morrow –
   Who knows? in joy or sorrow
We join thy dead, O Sea.

# The Boats of Sennen (Cornish Fisher-Girl's Song)

   The corn is in the shock,
   And the fish are on the rock,
And the merry boats go dancing out of Whitesand Bay,
   I hear the huer's cry,
   And I see the dappled sky,
And it minds me of the days that are long gone away.

   The corn was in the shock,
   And the fish were on the rock,
And the sea was all alive from the Wolf to Castle Treen,
   But the fog came down by night,
   And it hid the Longship's light,
And the men that went a-fishing never more were seen.

   The corn was in the shock,
   And the fish were on the rock,
When the boats went out from Sennen with the pilchard seine;
   But the morning broke so fair,
   And not a boat was there,
And the lad I love was with them and he came not back again.

   The corn is in the shock,
   And the fish are on the rock,
And the golden sun is gleaming on the Islands of the West;
   I hear the huer's cry,
   And I see the dappled sky,
And my heart is dead with sorrow for the lad I love the best.

# The Exile

There is wailing of the west wind on the land,
  There is lapping of the water on the beach,
There is sighing of the rushes in the sand,
  There is breaking of the breakers out of reach,
In the land that is mine own, the land of moor and down –
But I only hear the clanging roar of London Town.

On the lines of purple hills against the west,
  On the falling of the land towards the sea,
There are brakes of golden blossoms, where they rest
  'Mid the crimson of the heather on the lea,
In the land that is mine own, the land of flowery down,
While I gaze down upon the streets of London Town.

There is glitter of the sun upon the sea,
  As it lies in green and blue beneath the sky,
There is freedom in the salt air dashing free,
  On the white sails of the ships a-sailing by.
O sweet land that is mine own, thy tides go up and down –
While I but breathe the dirty smoke of London Town.

In the soughing of the south upon the waves,
  In the screaming of the gulls as they swoop round,
In the swirling rush of waters in the caves,
  In the cadence of the plover's lonely sound
I now hear the calling, and the wailing and the moan
Of poor lost souls upon the streets of London Town.

Oh for days of freedom spent in that dear land,
  One deep breathing of the salt from off the sea,
Glint of passing sun and shadow on the strand
  One soft murmur of the deep sea's melody!
It is Heaven on earth to me, this land of no renown; –
But I look down upon the streets of London Town.

**Ernest L.T. Harris-Bickford 1859–c.1924**

## Cornwall's Cliffs

See the cliffs, in craggy splendour,
  Tower magnificently high;
Kissed by breezes, cool and tender,
  Echoing sea-waves' shriek or sigh.

Rich in heather, steep, unbending,
  Deep descending, broad of brim!
Man athwart them wand'ring, wending,
  Feels the heart's-depths stirred in him.

Is he weary? yield they vigour;
  Is he languid? they will cheer;
Is he doomed to senseless rigour?
  They will give him comfort dear.

They will tell him how through ages
  They have borne the brunt of storm;
And that though old Ocean rages,
  They present a stalwart form.

They present a moveless barrier,
  So impregnable, supreme,
That the wind, destruction's carrier,
  Passes o'er them like a dream!


## Lander's Grave[1]

And is thy grave with jungle overgrown?
  And may no eye detect thy place of rest?
Canst thou not call some sheltered spot thine own,
  With flowers bright blooming o'er thy dauntless breast?

Martyr! I marvel as I think of thee,
  Removed from loving kindred and from home,
And wonder greatly how such thing can be,
  Afar, afar, across the whitening foam!

And must it thus continue? Dearth be thine?
  Are there no hearts that beat to make the spot
That holds thee beautiful? no thought benign
  Yet to be born to crown thy hapless lot?

Chief of thy time! of valorous enterprise!
  Much gentle kindness should be shown to thee;
Dear should thy grave be to all English eyes,
  And Cornish hearts, alive to chivalry!

Thy life was lost, investigation-led,
  Thy brave heart burned to open up new ways;
Death only claimed thy clay, – thou art not dead,
  Though closed on earth the sunshine of thy days.

And those who cherish men like Davy, Drake,
  Drew, Howe, and Raleigh, should not let thee lie
Supinely comfortless, but thought awake
  How best to draw to thee the passing eye.

Though sleeping far from Cornwall, Cornwall's son,
  In History's page thy name is graven deep,
Not midst thine own, but foes amid, were won
  Those laurels bright 'twas thine to form and keep!

And O! I trust such feeling yet will stir
  In Cornish hearts as shall re-echo wide,
And prove that thou hast many a worshipper
  Whose heart, at thought of thee, doth swell with pride.

God guard thee, Lander! in thy slumber lone,
  And breed the wish to re-invest thy grave
With fitting monument of carven stone,
  Near Santa Isabel – across the wave!

**James Dryden Hosken 1861–1953**

## Let Me Hear in My Verses

Let me hear in my verses the splashing of Cornish seas,
  Let me see the rock-pools fill with the fresh-coming tide,
Let me hear in my songs the sound of the wizard breeze
  Wailing across the moor, and haunting the dark hillside.

Land of lonely shadows, and lights from surges tossed,
  Land of the morning silence, land of the evening gloom,
Land of ancient races, long dead and gone, and lost,
  Land of the crying seabird, and ocean's far-heard boom.

Land of wailing voices and things that haunt the night,
  Of an eye that shines in darkness, and the hands of one who
                                                    flees,
Of storm round the Druid cromlech, and a mild and steadfast light
  Above the Celtic crosses seen far off from the seas.

Land of my songs, who art to me as to my life is the breath,
  Come and make my thoughts music, live and speak in my
                                                    rhymes,
Region of beauty and terror, meeting of life and death,
  Whose waters and breezes forget not the chants of twilight
                                                    times.


## When Our Seine Nets Are Dropped in the Bay

When our seine nets are dropped in the bay,
  And the pilchards come in from the deep,
And the silvery white-bait play
  On the waves that shoreward leap;
        The hearth is alight,
        And the cottage is bright,
And the village wakes up from its sleep.

O Bess shall have ribbons and shoes,
  And the wife a new bonnet and gown;
O it's not every haul that we lose
  When the nets to the bottom drop down;
        And the Ship Inn shall ring
        To the songs we will sing,
When we've sold all our fish in the town.

O safe in the cove are the fish,
    And all lend a hand at the haul;
Though the waves hurry in with a swish,
    Yet we hang to the nets one and all;
        All the village is here,
        And we pull with a cheer,
Watched by bright eyes that gleam 'neath a shawl.


## Porthleven

The brown sails tremble as the breeze
    Outside the harbour, takes the boat,
And over silent evening seas
        Towards the west we float.

Shadowy and dim the less'ning land
    A charmèd thing behind us lies,
O'er which the sun with gleaming wand
        Hath drawn the sleeping skies.

Shade after shade from light to dark,
    With scare perceptible decay,
Around the course of our frail bark
        Lingers the dying day.

And now 'tis gone, and high o'er head
    Night's thronging splendours flash and shine,
And thoughts of rapture and of dread
        At intervals are mine.

Far gleam the lights of Mullion – far
    Halzephron's[1] shadow clouds the deep
And bound with darkness, like a star
        Twinkles St Michael's Keep.

O, nights of wonder and of power,
    Be mine to prove your joy's again,
To crowd with years one mighty hour
        Upon the midnight main.

# Phran² of Goonhilly

What wight in western Cornwall strays
  'Mid old and unfrequented ways
And hears not of Goonhilly?
It is a wild and dreary down
That lieth north of Lizard town,
A place of bogs and boulders brown,
  And winds for ever chilly.

And yet, when summer skies are fair,
And nothing breaks the brooding air
  But far-off sound of ocean,
The solitary place can give
Emotions rare and fugitive,
That show the daily life we live
  A barren, blind commotion.

The magic sea on either hand
Hath cast a spell upon the land,
  Controlling change and nature;
Traditions gray and vanished things
Take shape in casual visitings,
Fair ladies, knights, and Cornish kings,
  And many a dwarfish creature.

Midway the down a cromlech stands,
Reared long ago by giant hands
  As told in antique story;
And some have gone on pilgrimage
To see the place where Phran the sage
Wore out his life from youth to age,
  Within that cromlech hoary.

He dwelt alone with solitude
And contemplation, in that rude
  And strange primeval dwelling;
Alone both night and day was he,
Alone with God, the stars and sea,
And all the thrilled immensity
  Of holy thought upwelling.

The walls of his gray home he traced
With starry charts, not yet effaced,
  And many a line and angle;
For it was said, he knew of things
Above the daily questionings

That haunt our life with erring wings,
  The spirit to entangle.

At times, when night was drawing nigh,
The wanderer saw against the sky
  The form of Phran outstanding,
And deemed it was a spirit form
Of lonely wilderness and storm,
Or in his fancy he would form
  A chief his host commanding.

None ever met him in the way,
And how he lived no man could say,
  And when he died none knew it:
When winter nights are dark and cold,
Beside the fire the tale is told,
How no one seeks that cromlech old,
  But he through life doth rue it.

The legends of a simpler age
Cling round the tale of Phran the sage,
  And linger round the ruin;
No hunter now will dare to trace
The crouching hare too near that place,
Where gorse and heath display their grace,
  The summer's earliest doing.

It may be, maddened by the world,
Or by wild passions hither hurled,
  He fled untruth and riot;
But howsoe'er the thing had been,
An influence hovers o'er the scene
Prompting high thought, and hopes serene,
  'Mid Nature's holy quiet.


# The Land of the West

She hath an ancient story,
  And stricken fields of fame,
A bright historic glory,
  A halo round her name.

Her heart's a moorland vastness,
  Her zone it is the sea;
A light above a fastness
  Her lure to liberty.

# Carminowe and Goonhylda[3]

Low burns the light in Carminowe,
  Its lonely towers in darkness lie;
And o'er the waters of the Loe
  Hangs a tempestuous sky.
Far down the creek, like souls in pain,
  The voices of the winds are heard,
Moaning and calling from the main;
  And now some restless bird
Starts from the dreary Forest side,
  With boding scream on rousing wings,
And skims the dimly glimmering tide;
  The while a spirit sings
Within the Druid ring of stones,
  That beetles o'er the evil lake –
"My throne is set on dead men's bones;
  Toll of the quick I take."

Lord Carminowe, alone is he
  Within his crumbling tower to-night,
He hears the moaning of the sea,
  The loos'ned tempest's might.
Thro' whistling crannies in the wall
  The night wind shakes the taper's flame,
And thro' the corridors doth call
  On chiefs of ancient fame.
Ah, evil days, Lord Carminowe,
  Brood o'er the last of that great line,
Whose chivalry, and glory low,
  'Mid taunt and scorn decline.
And thy betroth'd Goonhylda fair,
  Is held a prisoner by thy foe
Within St Michael's Mount, and there
  Craves aid of Carminowe.

There while that wretched Lord doth muse,
  His fancies rock'd by stormy sound,
An old retainer comes with news
  Of store of gold then found –
Of gems, and golden shields, and urns,
  And antique coin in glittering heaps,
And one great Ruby that outburns
  The Sun, when first he leaps
Upon the misty wall of dawn;
  And many other wondrous things,
The treasures of some mighty pawn

Paid by forgotten kings
To Carminowes in olden time,
    For Cornwall's rich and priceless ores;
When Carthage ruled in all her prime
    The queen of western shores.

Or more remote, when Egypt sent
    The dwellers by the dreamy Nile
From out the mystic orient
    To seek the western isle.
These treasures 'neath the oldest wall
    That night were by retainers found,
Who heard a voice of anguish call
    From out the haunted ground.
Lord Carminowe, like man in dream,
    Is dazed with joy beyond his wits:
He waves his torch, while golden gleam
    O'er gem and armour flits.
Lo! his great wealth hath come to him,
    To raise the fortunes of his line,
And rescue from a dungeon grim
    Goonhylda, the divine.

He buys the lances of the west,
    And leads his knights along the shore;
Fair hopes and fancies fill his breast,
    As dark, abrupt and hoar,
St. Michael's tower crown'd mount doth rise –
    A threat'ning form from out the wave,
And piled against the storm rent skies,
    Scowls on th' advancing brave.
Ah, me, Lord Carminowe, thy powers
    For three long days were tax'd in vain
To conquer those remorseless towers,
    And thy Goonhylda gain;
And then by treachery thy foe
    Had thee betray'd within his gate,
And all the line of Carminowe
    In thee was sunk by fate.

That night against the battlements
    Goonhylda stood with streaming hair,
Against the tempests moony rents
    The phantom of despair.
An aged monk beside her stood
    And strove to stay her frenzied flight;
Thrice gazed she on the ocean flood,
    Then leapt the tottering height.

Like to a flashing star she fell
  From battlement to that wild sea,
Whose foaming and Atlantic swell,
  Is fill'd with mystery –
With mystery, and memories
  Of many old forgotten things,
Of broken hearts, and loving eyes,
  And fair betrothal rings.

"Alas! when mortal man doth rule,"
  Thus sigh'd the monk above the wave –
"This Michael's hold – him falleth dool –
  Dool, and an evil grave."
Long ages after there were found
  Within a dungeon vaunted low,
An antique sword, a dusty mound,
  And crest of Carminowe.

# Ah! Gwen Carlyon[4] o'er This Heart

Ah! Gwen Carlyon o'er this heart
    You reign by beauty's right;
The panting spring with wak'ning start
    Before you opens bright.
All joys are yours, and night and day
    Like thoughts to you belong;
Fair queen of earth's divine array,
    And life's most haunting song.

Not time, nor place, nor life I know
    Beyond your reign of bliss;
No star to guide me but your brow;
    No honour but your kiss.
Then be my time, my place, my life,
    My star, my honour still,
And far from earth's unmeaning strife
    Let love work out its will.

# I Soon Shall Leave Those Eyes of Thine

I soon shall leave those eyes of thine,
  That love-lit smile no more shall see,
When other far-off scenes are mine
  Beside my native southern sea;
But in the north my heart abides,
  And through the days that are to come
Those eyes of thine will be my guides,
  That smile, a ray to draw me home.

To leave thee now, to leave thee now,
  In all thy love and beauty bright;
To leave the banquet in its glow
  Of burning joy, and seek the night;
And yet the night will quickly flee,
  My heart shall make it rich with song;
Those eyes of thine my stars shall be,
  That smile, a shield against all wrong.

Then ere we part, come heart to heart,
  And lip to lip in rapture press'd
We'll live one moment ere we part,
  To dwell with memory all the rest;
Thus let us part, and as I go,
  Oft turn to see thy last sweet smile;
But though my thoughts in music flow,
  My heart is breaking all the while.


# The Cornish Miner's Funeral

The furze is blooming on the silent moor,
And faintly falls the distant ocean's roar
Across the Wendron[5] hills; while overhead,
A point of music o'er his earthy bed,
The lark hangs singing songs of cloudless June
Enchanting all the drowsy afternoon.
But who are these with halting step and slow,
And heads dejected with an unfeigned woe?
The solemn hymn ascending to the sky,
The lamentation and the frequent sigh,
The serious miners closing round the bier
Proclaim a comrade's funeral drawing near,
Hark! clear and strong those sacred strains are heard,
That oft the deepest human chords have stirred.

"Though generations waste me, and decay
Eats all my outward form of man away;
Though years innumerable I sleep in dust,
No time, no power in Thee will shake my trust;
Thou, my Redeemer, livest, and at last
When rings through earth and sea the judgment blast,
Then, face to face before Thee shall I stand,
And own the power of Thy redeeming hand."

Garbed decently, the centre of the band,
Leading a little maiden by the hand,
See the fond wife, to whom no years restore
The service and the love she knew of yore.
Behind her, neat in suits she patched and turned
While hot her widowed heart within her burned,
Two rosy youngsters marked by every eye
Unconscious of their loss go toddling by.

To God's own keeping, He the only friend
Of fatherless and widow, we commend
This little company of friendless folk
Slow passing under sorrow's bitter yoke.

The Cornish mine has been the home of thought,
Of noble lives and hopes in darkness wrought:
Yea, formed by musing in the darkened deep,
Some master mind oft scaled heaven's beckoning steep.
Sometimes in wild Botallack's shafts and caves,
O'er which the deep Atlantic shoreward raves,
The sweet unconscious strains of song were born,
Or science taught some toiling mind forlorn:
Or near Redruth and Gwennap, many a time,
Unknown to science, and unskilled in rhyme,
How some grand soul religion there has sought
And through the lowliest life her wonders wrought.

Ah, vain the learning of the schools compared
To that self-trained intelligence he bared,
The sleeper, sung to his last earthly home,
When free on star-lit hill he oft would roam;
Or on some towering crag o'erhang the deep,
Or flash his vision on from steep to steep
Of perilous lonely heights, far hid away
From every sense awakened by the day.
No more the music of Isaiah's strain
Or Job's diviner note shall thrill his brain;
Nor deep in earth with straggling lights and dim
Will he awake the echoes with a hymn,
While standing reverend with bare heads around,
The miners gather to the well-loved sound.

Sing him to rest, each tender, faithful friend;
Hold to the faith that cries, "'Tis not the end."

Hold to the hope that whispers, "When life's way
Is travelled by you to its latest day,
The face that now has vanished from your sight
Will greet you in a land of joy and light,
Where tears are wiped away, and God's own breast
Welcomes the weary-hearted to its rest."


## Chant of a Cornish Exile[6]

Beautiful lies my land
As the shield of St Michael the victor,
Standing in silence and might
Against the loud thundering Atlantic;
Where the dark height of Bolerium
Frowns on the mountainous billows,
And calls in triumph aloud
To towering Penwith o'er the headlands,
Still to hurl back with might
The eternal war of the surges.

How like a warrior of old
He catches the thick-coming lances,
Driven by the furious ocean
Harmless against his dark armour;
For these he breaks and hurls back
Far out across the tempest,
Lit by the hills of foam
Churned up by the battle gigantic.

O Cornwall, dreamer of dreams
Dreams of the days of thy glory,
Days when the pennon of chivalry
Gleamed on thy hill-tops and beacons,
Days when the pilgrim knelt
By the cross on the roadside and worshipped;
And against the green of the oaks,
In the far-retiring valleys,
Shone the white form of Christ
Over the cell of the hermit.

Land of my heart, bourne of my dreams,
Fount of my song art thou, Cornwall;
Casket wherein my hopes
And my memories are hidden for ever.

Ah, who knows the heart of the exile
Severed from thee by the ocean,

As he paces an alien shore
Listening the chant of the billows,
While the clean wind-swept downs of St Cleer,
And the wide moors of Bodmin,
With the dark height of Caradon
Showing away to the eastward,
Rise to view like the landscape
Revealed by the lightnings of night!

O for the pleasant valleys
That wind in a golden shimmer
Of sunlight striking the oaks,
And the tough, smooth stems of the ash-trees,
And the sycamores lining the way
From the lone uplands to Looe,
And the deep-recessed nook of Polperro.

O for the light of thy streams, O Cornwall,
The swish of thy breezes;
O for the song of the lark
Singing to silent meadows.
O for the poetry haunting
Thy deep green lanes and thy roadsides,
Where in some ancient inn
With lattice embowered in roses,
Happy travellers rest,
And free from the stir of the world,
Gossip of far-off happenings
Throughout the perfumed day.


## One and All

Now hear me all the Cornish clan,
Each Grammar Grace and Uncle Jan,[7]
Who spring from that first Cornishman[8]
    Who long ago
Could sling a giant like a can
    O'er Plymouth Hoe.

I've got you all within my mind,
You gentle-hearted chields and kind;
And while I live I'll try and find
    Some bit of rhyme
To which old memories far behind
    Shall skip in time.

I've travell'd east, I've travell'd west,
I've seen the worst, and known the best;
But all the profit, joy or rest,
    I've known outside,
Within the pocket of my vest
    I well could hide.

But after all my journeys run,
And after all my labours done,
I'd like to know now, what I've won
    For all my pains –
Now tell the truth, as sure's a gun
    I've lost my gains!

I've lost my gains, Soas, lost them all,
By being Fortune's tennis ball;
I've fared far worse than Master Saul
    In Fate's dark passes,
He found a Kingdom – luck his thrall –
    I found his asses.

I've lost my all in realms afar,
By seeking fortune 'neath a star;
From youth's fair harbour, o'er the bar
    I set my sail
To gain in unknown seas, the scar
    Of fight and gale.

I've seen the tempest break its chain,
And darkly swoop across the main,
While mountain billows struck again
    The flying stars –
My skiff, that could no refuge gain –
    A wreck of spars.

Then while the lightnings show'd each board,
And through the vast the thunder roared,
I've held my breath to cry – O Lord!
    How long! – how long!
Till soft – a lull; and upward soar'd
    My heart in song.

And then my leaky craft to right,
And make her sit the waves more light,
I've worked to make her water-tight;
    And ease her beam
By throwing overboard my freight
    Of hope and dream.

Ah! countless bales of golden hopes
I've lowered o'er her side by ropes;
I've sank more dreams in those dark slopes
    Of howling sea
Than any twenty kings or popes
      Could e'er set free.

But what is life without some dream,
Or youth without some beck'ning beam? –
'Tis not to be, but just to seem
    A little blest –
For me – the path to heights supreme –
      And then the rest!

But what has this to do at all
With Cornwall and its "One and All?"
I thought some fancies down to scrawl
    Upon that text –
But since this chance is past recall
      I'll wait the next.

And yet this rhyme I cannot end
Without a word to each warm friend
Who loves the inside man to mend
    With Cornish pasty,
So let her rip, I'll not offend
      By being hasty!

O! Cornwall, land of sea and moor,
Of golden furze, and sparkling shore,
Of cream as thick as todge, and more
    Rich things beside
Than I can ever number o'er
      With proper pride.

Ah, Cousin Jack,[9] though half the earth
Makes games of your unbounded mirth –
You're nature's favourite from your birth,
    And wave and hill,
Within your soul have made a dearth
      Of many an ill.

I'd leave to fortune every dish,
If she would give me but this wish –
Good luck to copper, tin, and fish,
    The last, not least,
May lucky nets on sands still swish
      The pilchard feast!

O! Cornwall, land of heart and song,
May yet my days be full and long
Upon thy hills, and far along
     Thy dripping shores,
Where the great battle shout of wrong
     No longer roars.

Then one and all! on shore and main,
The beauty of our land maintain,
And shield her brow from every stain
     Of greed or fashion.
Until this love of her remain
     A holy passion.

# The Order of the World

My heart sinks when I look upon the world
  And see the wronger cased in evil might;
The bloody flag of hell at large unfurled,
  While vice and misery clothe themselves in night;
The cry of innocence, the growl of lust,
  Fair claims despised, and unjust avarice,
Merit and honour trampled in the dust,
  While sin and virtue are made casting dice,
Shook in the cup of Custom, held by Time,
  With all humanity to watch the game.
Time was when all injustice, woe and crime
  Were straight redressed by heroes of fair fame.
     O! that we had those old knights' chivalry,
     The wronged to succour, and the slave to free.

# The Sea of Life Doth Ebb

The sea of life doth ebb, and leave the strand
     Strewn with these wrecks of youth,
Which I stoop down and glean with patient hand;
The loud wave foams behind me, and a land
     Untravelled by my feet, and blank as night
      Opens upon my sight:
And evermore a weary voice of ruth
     Awakes love echoes on each sentinel height –
"O, life! O, time! where have ye hidden truth?"

# Song

Sink gently in the silent sea,
    Die slowly, slowly in the west;
Lull'd by the winds sweet minstrelsy
    To golden rest.

Thy wak'ning I shall view no more
    Behind the east's pale shimmering hills;
Ere thou dost rise the tale is o'er
    Of earthly ills.

## Arthur Quiller Couch 1863–1944

# The Planted Heel

By Talland Church[1] as I did go,
I passed my kindred all in a row;

Straight and silent there by the spade
Each in his narrow chamber laid.

While I passed, each kinsman's clay
Stole some virtue of mine away:

Till my shoes on the muddy road
Left not a print, so light they trod.

Back I went to the Bearers' Lane,
Begged the dead for my own again.

Answered the eldest one of my line –
'Thy heart was no one's heart but mine.'

The second claimed my working skill,
The third my wit, the fourth my will:

The fifth one said, 'Thy feet I gave;
But want no fleetness here in the grave.

'For feet a man need have no care,
If they no weight of his own may bear.

'If I own naught by separate birth,
What binds my heel e'en now to the earth?'

The dead together answered back –
'Naught but the wealth in thy knapsack.'

'Nay, then,' said I, 'that's quick to unload':
And strewed my few pence out on the road.

'O kinsmen, now be quick, resume
Each rag of me to its rightful tomb!'

The dead were silent then for a space.
Still I stood upright in my place.

Said one, 'Some strength he will yet conceal.
Belike 'tis pride of a planted heel?

'Man has but one perduring pride:
Of knowledge alone he is justified.

'Lie down, lie down by us in the sod:
Thou shalt be wise in the ways of God.'

'Nay, so I stand upright in the dust,
I'll take God's purposes all on trust.

'An inch of heel for a yard of spine, –
So give me again the goods that are mine!'

I planted my heel by their headstones,
And wrestled an hour with my kinsmen's bones.

I shook their dust thrice into a sieve,
And gathered all that they had to give.

I winnowed knowledge out of the heap:
'Take it,' I said, 'to warm your sleep.'

I cast their knowledge back on the sod,
And went on my journey, praising God.

Of all their knowledge I thought me rid:
But one little grain in my pack had hid. –

Now, as I go, myself I tell,
'On a planted heel man wrestles well.'

But that little grain keeps whispering me –
'Better, perhaps, on a planted knee.'

## Sonnet: Isles of Scilly

I saw Narcissus in a portico
  Leaning his ear toward the yellow bells
  Of his own flower, festooned, that from the shells
Voluted on the pavement, caught the low
Long echoes of an Archipelago
  Afar, beyond the pillared parallels
  Wherein a soft wind wound, and nothing else,
Between his shoulder and the afterglow.

Figure of bronze! Thou listenest alway:
  Ever for thee that lazy song beguiles.
But I must wake, and toil again, and pray;

And yet will come but rarely, and at whiles,
  The shout and vision of the sea-gods grey,
Stampeding by the lone Scillonian isles.


# The Harbour of Fowey

O The Harbour of Fowey
    Is a beautiful spot,
And it's there I enjowey
    To sail in a yot;
Or to race in a yacht
    Round a mark or a buoy –
Such a beautiful spacht
    Is the Harbour of Fuoy!

When her anchor is weighed
    And the water she ploughs,
Upon neat lemoneighed
    O it's then I caroughs;
And I take Watts's hymns
    And I sing them aloud
When it's homeward she skymns
    O'er the waters she ploud.

But the wave mountain-high,
    And the violent storm,
Do I risk them? Not Igh!
    But prefer to sit worm
With a book on my knees
    By the library fire,
Whilst I list to the brees
    Rising hire and hire.

And so, whether I weigh
    Up the anchor or not,
I am happy each deigh
    In my home or my yot;
Every care I resign,
    Every comfort enjoy,
In this cottage of mign
    By the harbour of Foy.

And my leisure's addressed
    To composing of verse
Which, if hardly the bessed,
    Might be easily werse.

And, the spelling I use,
        Should the critics condemn,
Why, I have my own vuse
        And I don't think of themn.

Yes, I have my own views:
        But the teachers I follow
Are the Lyrical Miews
        And the Delphic Apollow.
Unto them I am debtor
        For spelling and rhyme,
And I'm doing it bebtor
        And bebtor each thyme.

## Helford River

Helford River, Helford River,
  Blessed may ye be!
We sailed up Helford River
  By Durgan from the sea.

O to hear the hawser chain
  Rattle by the ferry there!
Dear, and shall we come again
  By Bosahan,
By wood and water fair?

All the wood to ransack,
  All the wave explore –
Moon on Calamansack,
  Ripple on the shore.

– Laid asleep and dreaming
  On our cabin beds;
Helford River streaming
  By two happy heads;

– Helford River, streaming
  By Durgan to the sea,
Much have we been dreaming
  Since we dreamed of thee.

Dear, and shall we dream again
  The one dream there?
  All may go if that remain
By Bosahan,
  And the old face wear!

## Celtic Perversity

When the Druids came to Cornwall crowned with oak and
                                                    mistletoe
All the gentry of the county bade the Druids scoot and go,
        In a language quite significant and terse;
        For the Cornishmen by nature are perverse;
Yet according to tradition they began a wondering,
For the kissing was appealing which the mistletoe did bring
And they dyed themselves in azure, in a shade as the lastest thing
        Which in a way was wonderful and strange,
        For the Cornishmen of all men hate a change;
But when the Phoenicians came and bartered bits of glass
For the Cornish tin in plenty, and the copper, and the brass,
It was plainly "nothing doing," for the Celt was not an ass!
        And of all things to this barter was averse,
        As is shown by this illuminating verse.

When St Joseph[1] came to Cornwall near two thousand years ago,
All the gentry of the county bade St Joseph sail and go,
        In a manner quite befitting gentlemen,
        In the language of the school of Tre, Pol and Pen;
Yet according to tradition soon with Joseph they did sing,
And they saw their dress of azure was a most unseemly thing,
And they got a taste for bathing, when he started christening,
        In the water which they were at first averse,
        When they took the plunge for better or for worse.
And so when the warlike Roman came and offered yellow gold
For the Cornish tin in plenty, then they were no longer cold,
And we find good business doing, as the writers writ of old;
        For the Cornishman by temperament is made
        Sympathetic to a free and easy trade.

When the Irish sailed to Cornwall sixteen hundred years ago,
All the Christian Celts in Cornwall bade the Irish Christians go.
        For the Cornishmen of all men hate a change,
        Which is not so very wonderful and strange;
And according to tradition, Teudar then a Cornish king,
And a Christian by profession, did a very fearful thing,
For he thrust the missionaries in a nasty boiling spring!
        For this Teudar was uncommonly perverse,
        And tradition says at times it was his curse.
But later when St Petrock, good St Piran, and St Ewe,

Came to Cornwall, then the Cornish made the greatest how-de-do
And we find they dined the Irish with their own good Irish stew,

And this too was a truly wondrous time,
As shown by this illuminating rhyme.


When St Neot toured the Duchy fifteen hundred years ago,
Many Cornishmen in Cornwall bade the Saxon Neot go.
    For the Cornishmen have ever stood aloof
    From sacerdotal censure or reproof.
But according to tradition Neot charmingly did sing
For he never cared a button – being friend of England's king,[2]
And he sang, "Oh, Irish brethren, is this now a seemly thing?
    I ask ye in my Anglo-Saxon verse,
    Are ye heretics, or infidels perverse?"
Then St Piran, and St Petrock, and St Issey, called the Good,
Built a house for good St Neot, by a murmuring stream and wood
With a spring in which St Neot, with his psalter, often stood!
    Which shows by this extremely learned verse,
    St. Neot had a fad, or something worse!


When King Edward sent to Cornwall some four hundred years
                                     ago,
Many Christian men in Cornwall bade his agents scoot and go;
    For the Cornishmen of all men were content
    To go the way their Christian fathers went;
And according to tradition they in anger cried: "A shame!
Give us back our old religion, not a thing without a name.
But a vulgar chitter chatter mumming like a Christmas game!"
    For the Cornishmen of all men weren't the folk
    To treat religion as if it were a cloak!
But according to the story, Edward ridiculed their prayer,
For he sent his provost marshall, he who dined with Bodmin's
                                         mayor,[3]
And who went and hanged him after! as an ordinary affair!
    In a manner unexpected, and in truth
    As callous as the marshall was uncouth!


When Wesley turned to Cornwall – that's now many years ago,
All the curates, priests, and deacons, bade this good reformer go,
    And the laymen too, were more than all content
    To join the clergy's cry against dissent.
But now we know the story of the county's vicious plight,
Empty churches, plural livings, plainly pictured Cornwall's blight,
"Drunk for twopence, straw for nothing!" advertised a tavern
                                         wight
    The vilest age that England's ever seen,
    Which Wesley came with godliness to clean.
And now we know no more indeed the folk or clergy tried,

To stem dissent where Wesley went, and that on every side
They followed him, they sang with him, they prayed with him and
cried!

     The very men who came to scoff and play,
     Now played with him, and sped him on the way.


## Mary of Halveggan Down

    Ding, dangle, dong, ding,
    Saint Mewan Bells ring;
For 'tis merry to-day at Halveggan Down;
For Mary May Hooper and Cappen Joe King
Are marryin' and ridin' to Los'withiel town,
    And Hancock is drivin'
    With silken bows flyin'
    And clay pits are hootin'
    And clay men are shootin'
    From Stents to Carthew,
    'Tis a rare how de do;
    And guns are goin' rat tat,
    From Goonmarth to Greensplat;
And on to Treverbyn the claymen now sing;
"Here's luck to our Mary, and Cappen Joe King;
    Now married to-day
    And now on their way,
For a beano to Los'withiel Town."

"Then here's to our Mary, and Cappen Joe King,
Then out with it, fellows, and lustily sing;
    Not a girl in Saint Mewan,
    From Sticker to Trewoon,
    Beats Mary of Halveggan Down."

    Ding, dangle, dong, ding,
    Treverbyn bells ring;
For over the hills from Halveggan Down,
Comes Mary May Hooper and Cappen Joe King,
In a mighty smart kerridge to Los'withiel Town.
    And hark at the hootin'
    The racket and the shootin';
    Now Caudledown "knacker"
    Is going like a cracker;
    And the boys are all shoutin'
    This is a dry outin';
    Bring toddy and beer,
    For Cap'n is here.

And now with a chorus, Treverbyn boys sing;
And out you get, Mary, and Cappen Joe King
 And now roar "hurray,
 For Mary to-day,
 Mary of Halveggan Down."


 Pit, patter, rum, pum,
 Goes cornet and drum;
For Stenalees Band is come over the Down;
And Mary is dancin' with Cappen Joe King,
And handsome is she in her gabardine gown.
 And the bandsmen are playin'
 "Oh that we were mayin',"
 And gay is the dancin'
 The trippin' and prancin'!
 And Hancock is shoutin'
 "Now this is an outin'!"
 And maidens are skippin'
 Their partners outstrippin';
And merry the bells of Treverbyn now ring;
And Mary is happy – and Cappen Joe King
 Cries out "Stenalees,
 Play 'Hensbarrow Breeze'
Till they hear it on Halveggan Down."


 Ding, dangle, dick, dock,
 'Tis six by the clock;
And all away homeward from Los'withiel Town,
Comes Mary May Hooper, and Cappen Joe King,
While the sundown is paintin' lone Halveggan Down.
 And Hancock is laughin',
 And Cappen is chaffin',
 The clay pits are hootin',
 And claymen are shootin',
 Right on to Carthew
 'Tis a rare how de do;
 And crackers go rat tat
 From Carthew to Greensplat;
And all along downlong the claymen so sing:–
"Here's luck to our Mary and Cappen Joe King;
 Now married to-day,
 And now on their way,
Straight homelong to Halveggan Down."


 Ding, dangle, dick, dock,
 'Tis ten by the clock;
And Hancock is feelin' his way o'er the Down.

And Mary is laughin', and Cappen Joe King
Is kissin', and jokin' and playin' the clown.
    And Hancock is swearin'
    As the hosses go tearin'
    Down Halveggan Moor
    With racket and roar!
    And then with a thump
    Goes bumpetty bump,
    The kerridge all flop,
    By Berriman's shop!
While Cappen keeps laughin', as the boys come around:–
"Now out you get, Cappen, and, boys, raise a sound,
    For Cappen Joe King,
    And Mary we'll sing,
Now comin' from Los'withiel Town."

"Then here's to our Mary, and Cappen Joe King,
And out with it, fellows, and lustily sing:
    Not a girl in Saint Mewan,
    From Sticker to Trewoon,
Beats Mary of Halveggan Down."

## W. Herbert Thomas 1866–1951

# All Hail! Old Cornwall!

O Cornwall! rocky land where "strangers"[1] dwell,
  Thy scenes inspire and cheer thy favour'd sons,
From Land's End, where the echoing breakers swell,
  To where the Tamar's placid river runs;
And o'er wild oceans, in remotest lands,
  The exiled ones who hold thy memory dear,
Would link with us in love, by clasping hands,
  And swell the chanting of thy praises here!

Among thy verdant glens the winding streams
  Dance joyously, with sunny smiles illum'd;
And lovers wander, wrapp'd in fairy dreams,
  Beneath the trees with clust'ring foliage plumed:
The lark mounts high amid pellucid air,
  O'er valleys nestling 'neath the tow'ring hills,
And pours aloft a flood of music rare,
  As pure as pearly dew which earth distils.

Around thy rocky shores the billows break
  In gentle emerald curves on sand and shell;
Or caverns' groans and muffled roar awake –
  The sailors' requiem and funeral knell.
Along the beetling cliffs Time's fierce assaults
  Have sear'd and hollow'd their resisting base;
But till the circling world God's herald halts,
  No power thy majesty shall dare efface!

O Cornwall! On the scroll of history
  Thy name is writ in ancient characters,
Until we reach the veil of mystery,
  Where truth is hid, and speculation errs.
Aggressive nations cross'd the watery main
  To claim thy min'ral treasure for their prize;
And bloody battle-fields, and warriors slain,
  Awoke exultant shouts and heart-wrung cries.

Trace back a thousand years – yea, thousands more,
  And there we learn from legends that thy fame
Drew bold Phoenicians from the Spanish shore,
  And warlike Greek and Roman later came.
Perchance the metals from thy murky mines
  Adorn'd the temple rear'd by Solomon,[2] –
That Eastern sage whose crystal wisdom shines,
  Though crumbling ruins mark the glory gone!

Still toil thy hardy miners for the tin
  By Nature stor'd within her bowels deep;
With rolling waves o'erhead, and pent within
  The heated ground, half-naked heroes creep.
Death's shadowy form stalks, silent, as they swing
  The hewing pick, with arms like iron bars;
To quiv'ring threads of life they fearless cling,
  'Twixt hollow Earth and Heaven's eternal stars!

And gallant seamen skirt thy storm-swept shore,
  Nor fear the tempest's wrath or lightning's flash,
As in their tiny barques they scud before
  The sobbing wind, while waters fiercely dash.
Mark how the silver fishes writhe and gleam,
  Within the meshes caught, – a harvest rare!
Thy fisher sons, how joyous now they seem,
  As shouts and merry laughter fill the air!

In golden fields, where waves the ripen'd corn,
  The husbandmen wield scythes or bind the sheaves:
How light their hearts when filling Plenty's horn;
  When crops are blighted, how each spirit grieves!
Thy marts are throng'd, and Trade's deep hum is heard;
  Thy artisans ply busily their tools;
Thy halls with learning and with work are stirr'd,
  From council chambers to the children's schools.

And now, O Cornwall, think of those bright names
  In Science, Art, and Literature enrolled, –
Thy giants who, unmov'd by flood or flames,
  Their life's work wrought, their stirring message told!
Fell Superstition fled before their march;
  Light dawn'd, and stream'd into our waiting minds;
They rear'd o'er Beauty's shrine a rainbow arch,
  And fadeless laurel now each forehead binds!

Look now, proud Cornwall, o'er the surging sea!
  Behold the footprints traced on foreign soil!
In every land where thriveth Freedom's tree,
  Thy wand'ring sons still roam and bravely toil!
They delve for gems to deck a monarch's crown;
  They strive for bread to feed their cherish'd ones;
Pray God, they never may stoop basely down
  To shame, which noble manhood ever shuns!

Join hands, ye Cornish lads, across the main!
  Let Asia clasp Columbia's outstretch'd hand!
Come forth, Australia! Swell the glad refrain!

And touch the fringe of Afric's golden strand!
Swift o'er the boundless ocean rings the call!
  The mystic girdle round the world is cast!
Shout now with thund'rous voices "One and All"!
  All hail! Old Cornwall! May thy glory last!


# Entombed![3]

Deep down in the heart of the sunless mine,
  In the bowels of Dolcoath deep,
Heroes are toiling with might and main
  While the upper world is asleep;
And the hewing pick and the grinding saw,
  And dynamite's thundering sound,
Are heralds of hope to the hapless men
  Entombed in the murderous ground.

Half a mile deep in the Cornish mine,
  Away from the ocean air,
Away from the psalm of the singing bird
  And the odour of blossoms fair, –
Ride down the shaft to a sunless hell,
  Swung by a quivering rope,
Then, to the spot where the avalanche fell,
  Through the weird galleries grope!

Brave are the men of the ancient mine,
  Brave as the lion's heart,
Staking their lives 'gainst a golden coin –
  The wage of the white-slave's mart!
Tender as babes to babes are they,
  Yet bold as warriors can be,
And dauntless toil by the tide of death
  That rolls to Eternity!

They gaze on its waters without dismay,
  And its spectral pilots grim,
As they swing the pick and the mighty sledge
  By the flame of the candle dim –
As they swing the sledge and uprear the trunks
  Of the giant forest "balks,"
And hold in check the threat'ning mass
  In whose shadow stern Death stalks.

In the subterranean prison-mine
  Have these human strugglers worked,

While in poisoned air and exploding charge
　　A thousand dangers lurked.
They have scooped the copper and glistening tin
　　And the shining silver too,
Till the tunnels, seventy miles and more,
　　Have pierced Earth's bowels through.

And the danger grows with the flight of years,
　　And stouter the hearts of the men,
And with jest and laugh they labour there,
　　Each band in its rocky den;
For the lash of Want and the voice of Love
　　Nerve their arms, like tempered steel,
And though Death's keen sword by a thread is held,
　　No fear does its threat reveal.

One moment they toil 'neath the timbered roof
　　To strengthen its bending prop,
Then a warning crack – 'tis "a God-send" – comes,
　　And the trickling fragments drop:
An instant more – and the loosened mass
　　Crashes down like an avalanche,
While the whirling wind smites the miners brave
　　As a gale smites a broken branch.

By the current strong some are swiftly borne
　　To the tunnel's shelt'ring arch,
And behind them massive rocks are hurled
　　By the wind's unbridled march;
But eight brave men are there entombed
　　In a grave where horrors dwell,
And the sound of their comrades' ringing tools
　　Seems, alas, but a funeral knell.

The moments pass and the hours speed on,
　　And a day of anguish flies,
Then blinding tears and madd'ning fears
　　Supplant the hope that dies, –
But, hark! – from the darkness of the tomb
　　Comes a faint, sepulchral voice –
One is praising the Lord in the awful gloom!
　　He is crushed, but can still rejoice!

How the strong men weep! How they shout their joy!
　　But his comrades? Do they live?
Ah! *"God and myself alone are here"* –
　　Is the answer he must give:
Then he sings glad hymns till his life dies out

Ere deliverance can be given,
But the Christian's God is with him still
  Where the sun-lit clouds are riven!

Out from the tomb comes another voice –
  The voice of the Cornish lad –
And again the sound of his cheery words
  Makes many a sad heart glad:
Out from the tomb where the dead men dwell,
  Out from the gloom of Night,
He comes at last with a smile of joy
  To liberty and light!

Muffle the drum for the soldier brave,
  Struck from life's muster roll,
Fire a volley of prayers aloft
  While the deep church-bells toll.
They and their comrades, frail and strong,
  Rest till the trump shall sound,
When the dead shall rise from the troubled sea
  And from every graveyard mound.

Soft may the tears of the mourners fall –
  Tears for the peaceful dead –
Which mother and widow and fatherless child
  In their calamity shed.
Sorrowing ones! look away to the skies –
  Hark! for the voice rings clear –
"Follow the light that ascends to Heaven –
  *God and myself are here!*"

# In a Cornish Lane

The gossamer nets of the cobwebs had captured
        the jewelled rain,
And the bees were burdened with honey of flowers
        in the field and lane,
The bees were as glossy as velvet, and the cobwebs
        sparkled and swung,
And the chalice of white convolulus to its twining
        tendril clung.

The hedges were draped with creepers, with purple
        and golden blooms –
Rich tapestries woven by magic in Nature's
        mysterious looms,

And splashes of wine-tinted heather illumined the
      furze and the grass,
While the roadside stream, 'neath the oak-boughs,
      rolled on like melodious glass.

The world had seemed aged and barren when I left
      the town's dull streets,
Till I felt the green turf springing 'mid the brakes
      of Marguerites,
Till the buoyant breezes met me, and the pulsing
      songs of birds
Were mingled with the lowing of meadows'
      sauntering herds.

The joy that moves the butterfly to wave its
      speckled wings,
The gladness of the skylark as its roundelay
      its sings,
Was mine as I heard the music of the waves of
      mellowing grain,
As the perfumes of hay and clover was swept
      through the Cornish lane.

## The Gurnard's Head

Weary of drudgery, hard sounds and idle tales,
I roamed where tinkling rivulets, and streams
That hold the speckled trout, catch sunny gleams,
And perfume from late hawthorn buds regales;
And passed forget-me-nots in ferny dales,
Grey mossy rocks, hedgerow whose turf-slope teems
With trailing brambles, and sweet grass that seems
To wait the mowing scythe. Then left green vales
And trod brown moors, where gaunt grey carns uprear
Wild jagged heads, and boulders stud the heath,
Until loomed forth broad cliffs and headland sheer,
'Round whose weird base in awful grandeur wreathe
Mad roaring waves, whose hell-song wakened Fear,
Who drove me from the black storm's rending teeth.

# Sunset from Bodmin Beacon

Pent in an atmosphere of horrid crime,
The clouded day's dark burden heavier grew,
And, freedom gained, Desire's magnet drew
My footsteps beaconward, where peaceful chime,
From grey church tower, marked the flight of time.
O'er the green summit twilight breezes blew,
And 'round her wearied form the gipsy drew
Her shielding tent, near youths who often climb
The grassy heights to chase the bounding ball.
Through sombre clouds a ragged streak of fire
Broke, widened, blazed till rose-suffused were all
The purple skies, madhouse and prison dire,
And ruddily the dreary workhouse wall
Shone 'neath the dying son's grand phoenix-pyre.

**Anonymous [published 1869]**

## Lines on the Terrible Accident at the Old Delabole Slate Quarries, 1869

'Twas in the parish of St Teath,
   A place call'd Delabole,
Where fifteen persons met their death,
   by an untimely call.

On Wednesday, April twenty-first,
   Without a warning given,
A dreadful accident occurred –
   Men from their work were driven.

Near four hundred men and boys,
   Were at the works employ'd
In raising slate from day to day,
   Where many are destroy'd.

A papote head[1] with awful crash
   Fell down three hundred feet
And carrying with it tons of slate
   Did bury all beneath.

Some did escape miraculously
   An awful sudden death
While six were injured very much
   And nearly lost their breath.

When down it fell, the dreadful noise
   Was heard for miles around
And hundreds hasten'd to the spot –
   An awful scene they found.

Some wives and mothers gathered there
   And sons and daughters too,
Whose lamentations rent the air,
   They knew not what to do.

Dear little children cried in vain,
   "Oh, is my father dead?
   Oh, is he buried in the pit?
   Who now will give us bread?"

And mothers wept for sons whose fate
   Was then for ever seal'd

And wives for husbands cried aloud
    And their said fate bewailed.

Ten thousand tons of slate and stone,
    Lay on some victims there,
While others crush'd with heavy logs
    Were to the surface near.

Assistance came; but ah! too late;
    Much time did pass away,
Before the bodies were took out,
    From where in death they lay.

Six wives are left to mourn the loss
    Of husbands they loved dear,
And nineteen little children too
    For fathers shed a tear.

John Bone, Joe Hosking, William Toms,
    Tom Avery, James Penfound
Were single men who met their death
    With weeping friends around.

Michell, Langdon, Curtice, Taylor,
    Abbot and Prout also
With William Rowe all married men
    Leave families in great woe.

Thomas and William Langdon too,
    Two little brothers dear
And Fanny Wallis single woman,
    They all lay buried there.

O let us hope in heaven above,
    Again they all shall meet,
Parents and children and dear friends
    All safe at Jesu's feet.

May everyone a warning take,
    And for the end prepare,
For oh! how soon our life is gone,
    And death how very near.

Now in the silent grave they're laid,
    Until the judgement day.
O, may they hear the Saviour say,
    "Ye blessed come away."

## Annie E. Argall c.1876–c.1916

## The Charm of Beauty

How strangely sweet it is to note our world,
Apparently more lovely day by day!
And yet we know the change is not around,
But in ourselves. Nature has ever held
In her fair bosom many a mystery,
A hidden power of wondrous loveliness.
Yes, as the years pass on, and seasons change,
In each new opening flower afresh we note
Evidence of a lovely harmony.
The mystic growth of every budding tree
The soft green grass glist'ning with morning dew,
Late autumn varied tints and ruddy glows,
Now purely fair with all-entrancing charm
These in good sooth appear! And yet again,
The dawn of day, the twilight's shadowy hour,
The peaceful beauty of the river-path,
Old restless Ocean with his myriad waves
Fringed with the gleaming sand of many a shore,
These several scenes, widely diversified,
Each in its point of pleasure singular,
Strike new interest our awakened sight.


## The Fal

O, lovely Fal, whose wooded banks
To thy fair self give wondrous grace,
Of thee, loved stream, I fain would speak,
And having power, thy path would trace,
As flowing onward day by day,
Gently thou glidest on thy way.

Thou, changing ever, yet the same
To me, whose memory loves to rove
Along thy winding silvery course;
Around thy path I oft have wove
Sweet thoughts of pleasures past and gone,
When Love's fair sunlight o'er me shone.

As I, in frail and simple craft,
Down on thy heaving breast did glide;
In the glad transport of those hours

I dreamt not of what might betide, –
I had no thought for care or grief,
Or that life's joys would be but brief.

But those were days that now are past,
Though ling'ring in my memory yet,
Sweet joyous hours of honeyed bliss
That could I, I would ne'er forget,
For they are graven on my heart,
And in my dreams still bear a part.

List! gentle river, to my song,
And bear it onward to the sea;
Accept the tribute I would bring,
The meed of praise I grant to thee.
Flow on, O Fal, with this refrain,
Ye rippling waves, take up the strain.

**Anonymous [Ms 1913]**

## The Clay Strike[1] – the White Country Dispute

Perhaps it's interesting, and I guess that you would like
to hear an account of the Cornish Clay Strike:
Well, the men at Carne Stents were first to down tools,
And for taking that action were counted as fools.

But as you see their policy proved a blessing in disguise,
and has proved to the world that they were really wise,
Virginia men were next, and they had the nerve
and around the Fal Valley they all did serve.

To Kernick and Trethosa their course then they took
and down in those pits the crowd did look;
But the men were ignorant of the union resolution.
The great problem to them simply had no resolution.

Well then, friend, I think that they passed by Goonvean,
and held a great meeting at the bottom of Nanpean.
The organisers went there the strikers to meet.
They stood on the hedge and the man on the street.

At Foxhole we settled next morning to meet
The old scheme of wages we had to defeat;
For wages at present only just keep us alive
and now we are determined to reach "twenty five".

The course we then took was a place called Lanjeth,
And when we got there we were just out of breath,
But whilst waiting there a kind of friend we found,
Who opened his gate and in the field we sat down.

By the leaders, on the ground, some speeches were given,
And by the time they had done, the clock struck eleven.
After some consultation as to the course we should take
The men were unanimous for Blackpool to make.

In the China Clay area the motors are near flying,
To starve out the men the employers are trying,
But the Cornish are solid and determined to fight
To get the twenty-five shillings which they think is their right.

The world is now watching with an anxious eye,
To help these gallant claymen we hope you will try.

There is just one word more and then I have done –
Please give a donation to the Strike Relief Fund.

It is my pleasure, dear friends, to write part number two
of the China Clay Strike, which we have passed through.
Well after a month's struggle it commenced to rain
So the employers did their utmost to get back their men.

For these heavy showers helped fill in the pits
And just frightened the poor fellows into fits.
Then the next move was to import some hundred of police
Who would have us to believe they were sent to keep peace.

So all through the dispute ran the spirit of peace
Until it was broken by the Glamorgan police
Who I imagine fell in love too much with the barrel
And then John Barleycorn soon induced them to quarrel.

The Glamorgan police were all watching their tricks,
And demanded the pickets to give up their sticks,
When they caught a small number down in a by-lane,
They acted like demons or men gone insane.

Poor Vincent, our leader, was the first they attacked,
Was trundgeoned and batoned and his poor head they cracked;
I suppose they then left him by the roadside for dead
But they couldn't kill his spirit though they opened his head.

Well, six weeks had passed, and I would just like to note
That we decided to ballot and let the men vote;
The men were out against their will was the constant report,
So we wanted to the public 'twas a false report.

After taking their vote proved twasn't so;
To go to work two thousand two hundred and fifty eight said "No".
To go back on the old conditions this was the best,
One five hundred and sixty-eight voted yes.

Well, after ten weeks of hard fighting, we decided to retreat,
But some may claim it to be a defeat,
We are not downhearted, Boys, no not yet,
For an advance in wages we hope soon to get.

So boys join the workers union
And win the victory next time,
And if you'll promise to do so, why then I'll end my rhyme,
To see you all in the union is just what we would like,
Then we could settle by arbitration and thus avoid a strike.

**Anonymous [published 1919]**

# The Levant Mine Disaster[1]

St Just, Pendeen, and Neighbourhood
Will never forget the day
When thirty-one poor Miners
Were suddenly carried away.

This fearful accident occured,
On Monday at Levant,
And many a home is fatherless
Through this terrible event.

The Man Engine was at fault, they say:
Whilst bearing human freight,
Though very near the surface smashed –
And sent them to their fate.

The awful strenuous hours that passed
Whilst bringing up the dead
And rescuing the wounded,
The thought we almost dread.

There were many willing helpers
Came over from Geevor Mine,
To help the rescuing parties
Which was merciful and kind.

The Doctors too, must have our thanks
For attentiveness and skill,
In succouring wounded comrades
Brought to the surface very ill.

The Parson and the Minister
Both rendered yeoman aid,
To alleviate the sufferers
Christian diligence displayed.

Now in conclusion let me say
To rich as well as poor
Remember the Widows and Orphans
Of those that's gone before.

# Biographies and sources

### Andrew Boorde c.1500–c.1560

Very little is known about the life of Boorde, only that he studied medicine and was imprisoned for some time in the Tower of London. His most influential work was the *Fyrst Book of the Introduction of Knowledge*, dedicated to Mary Tudor and published in 1547.

*Iche Cham a Cornyshe Man*. F.J. Furnivall (ed.) (1870) *The Fyrst Book of the Introduction of Knowledge,* Oxford: Oxford University Press.

### Nicholas Roscarrock c.1548–1634

Roscarrock was born at Roscarrock in the parish of St Endellion in North Cornwall. He was a Cornish Catholic who was persecuted and imprisoned in the Tower of London. His greatest work was his stories of British and Irish saints, of which the Cornish section was one part. He may be seen as one of Cornwall's earliest hagiographers.

*A Sonnet*. Nicholas Roscarrock, *Lives of the Saints*. MS Add. 3041, Cambridge.
*A Friendly Warning About Saints.* Ibid.
*Of Saint Aaron.* Ibid.

### Richard Carew 1555–1620

Carew was born at Antony House near Torpoint in East Cornwall. A scholar, historian, poet and soldier, his greatest work was his *Survey of Cornwall*. Writing at a time when the Cornish language began to decline, he embraced the shift to English, in his view to be welcomed.

*Prosopopeia*. Richard Carew (1769 [1602]) *The Survey of Cornwall, and an Epistle concerning the Excellencies of the English Tongue*, Penzance: J. Hewett.
*The Well of St Keyne.* Ibid.
*The River Lynher.* Ibid.
*Epitaph for John Arundell.* Ibid.
From *A Herring's Tail*. Richard Carew (1598) *A Herrings Tayle: Containing a Poeticall Fiction of Divers Matters Worthie of Reading*, London: Matthew Lownes.
*Full Thirteen Five of Years*. Davies Gilbert (ed.) (1838) *The Parochial History of Cornwall*, Vol 4, London: J. B. Nichols and Son. Found in Appendix XIV.

### Michael Drayton 1563–1631

Drayton was born at Hartshill in Warwickshire and is most famous for his historical and topographical verse. He wrote a poem on the battle of Agincourt (1627) but his greatest work is the *Poly-Olbion* (1622). Drayton appears to have had a life-long interest in Cornwall: in 1598 he wrote a play entitled *Connan, Prince of Cornwall*.

From *First Song, Poly-Olbion*. Davies Gilbert (ed.) (1838) *The Parochial History of Cornwall*, Vol. 4, London: J.B. Nichols and Son. Found in Appendix VIII.

## Sidney Godolphin 1610–1643

Godolphin was born at Godolphin Hall, Helston. He was a Cornish Royalist and was killed at Chagford in Devon during the Civil War.

*Meditation on the Nativity*. W. Dighton (ed.) (1931) *Sidney Godolphin: Poems*, London.
*Song*. Ibid.
*Constancy*. Ibid.
*Fair Friend, 'Tis True Your Beauties Move*. Ibid.
*On Sir F. Carew*. Ibid.
*Constant Love*. Ibid.

## Thomas Hogg 1777–1835

Hogg was born in Kelso in Scotland, but for most of his life was a teacher at Truro Grammar School. He died in London.

*Godolphin*. W. H. K. Wright (ed.) (1896) *West-Country Poets: Their Lives and Works*, London: Elliot Stock.
*Witchcraft*. Thomas Hogg (1827) *The Fabulous History of Cornwall,* Truro: E. Heard.
*Fairies*. Ibid.

## Humphry Davy 1779–1829

Davy is best known for the invention of the miner's safety lamp. He was born in Ludgvan, near Penzance, eventually becoming a professor of chemistry at the Royal Institution in London. He was a friend of Coleridge and Wordsworth.

*In Ludgvan Churchyard*. Alison Pritchard (ed.) (1978) *Davy as Poet*, Penwith: Penwith District Council.
*The Sons of Genius*. John Ayrton Paris (1831) *The Life of Humphry Davy*, London: Henry Colburn and Richard Bentley.
*Ode to St Michael's Mount*. Ibid.
*The Tempest*. Ibid.
*Mount's Bay*. Ibid.
*The Song of Pleasure*. Ibid.

## George Woodley 1786–1846

Woodley was born in Dartmouth in Devon, but lived for much of his life in Truro. He first came to Cornwall to promote the work of the SPCK (Society for Promoting Christian Knowledge), but eventually became editor of the *Royal Cornwall Gazette*.

*Ode to Cornubia*. George Woodley (1819) *Cornubia: A Poem in Five Cantos,* Truro: Mitchell and Co.
*Roche Rock and Hermitage*. Ibid.
*Botallack*. Ibid.

## Henry Quick 1792–1857

Quick was born in Zennor in West Cornwall, and after the death of his father, he and his mother were forced to beg in the streets. He took odd jobs and sold brooms before his poetry began to be published in broadsheets. Much of his verse treats the theme of 'disasters', very popular with broadsheet readers. He is one of Cornwall's most remarkable literary phenomena.

*The Life and Progress of Henry Quick of Zennor*. Henry Quick (1836) *The Life and Progress of Henry Quick of Zennor*, Penzance: T. Vigurs.
*The Death of Pascoe Semmens, 1826*. Henry Quick (1826) *Broadsheet of a Copy of Verses on the Melancholy Accident and Sudden Death of Pascoe Semmens of Trazza in Ludgvan, Who Was Killed by Lightning in a Thunderstorm at Castle-Dennis-Downs on 9 June 1826, Aged 29 Years.*

*Acrostic on John Verrant of St Hilary, 1835*. Henry Quick (1835) *Acrostic on John Verrant of St Hilary, 1 December 1835* (MS at Penlee Museum, Penzance).
*The Death of John Martyns, 1836*. Henry Quick (1836) *A New Copy of Verses on the Fatal Accident and Death of John Martyns, a Poor Young Man of Ludgvan*. Penzance: Huthnance.
*John Uren of Boscrowan, 1847*. Henry Quick (1847) *Broadsheet of a New Copy of Verses Composed on the Memory of our Late Deceased Neighbour John Uren*. St Ives: R.D. Rodda.
*William Thomas of Boswednack*. Henry Quick (1822) *Broadsheet on William Thomas of Boswednack*, Penzance: Rowe.
*Our Cornish Drolls Are Dead*. William Bottrell (ed.) (1870) *Traditions and Hearthside Tales of West Cornwall: First Series*. Penzance: W. Cornish.

## John Tabois Tregellas 1792–1863

Tregellas was born in St Agnes, where his family had lived for many generations. In his day he was a popular author and lecturer, celebrated for his understanding of Cornu-English and humorous narratives.

From *St Agnes Bear Hunt*. John Tabois Tregellas (c.1863) *Cornish Tales*. Truro: Netherton and Worth.
From *Rozzy Paul and Zacky Martin*. Ibid.

## William Sandys 1792–1874

Sandys' pseudonym was Uncle Jan Trenoodle and the poem here was originally published under that name. He was educated at Westminster School (1800–1808) and became a solicitor. He later became the commissioner of affidavits in the Stannary Court of Cornwall, though is perhaps most famous for his work on Cornish Christmas carols and music.

*Visit to Lunnon*. Uncle Jan Trenoodle (1846) *Specimens of Cornish Provincial Dialect*, London: John Russell Smith.

## Francis Hingeston 1796–1841

Hingeston was born in St Ives and educated at Truro Grammar School. He was a man of leisure, who wrote many poems for his lady friends. His major poetic interest was in the Cornish landscape.

*Sonnet Written at the Land's End*. W.H.K. Wright (ed.) (1896) *West-Country Poets: Their Lives and Works*, London: Elliot Stock.

## Charles Taylor Stephens 1796–1863

Stephens was a rural postman covering the area from St Ives to Zennor. The poems appear to be have been published after he was invalided out of his job, and he aimed to earn a living by them. Another work, *Chimes from the Lapstone and the Lament of St Ia, a Poem* was planned, but never published.

From *The Chief of Barat-Anac*. C. Taylor Stephens (1862) *The Chief of Barat-Anac and other Poems, Songs &c*, St Ives: W. Kernick.

## John Abraham 1798–c.1870

Abraham was born in Liskeard, educated in Lostwithiel and set up a business there. His poetry shows a fascination with the Cornish landscape, Bodmin Moor in particular.

*The Barren Mountain*. W.H.K. Wright (ed.) (1896) *West-Country Poets: Their Lives and Works,* London: Elliot Stock..

## Robert Stephen Hawker 1803–1875

The poet and mystic Robert Stephen Hawker was born in Plymouth and studied at Pembroke College, Oxford. From 1834 he was the Vicar of Morwenstow in North Cornwall and assisted in the rescue of numerous shipwrecked mariners along the treacherous coast. A critic of Methodism and industrialisation, he converted to Catholicism a few hours before he died.

*The Song of Western Men*. C. E. Byles (ed.) (1904) *R. S. Hawker: Cornish Ballads and Other Poems*, London: John Lane, the Bodley Head.
*The Sea*. Ibid.
*The Silent Tower of Bottreau*. Ibid.
*The Western Shore*. Ibid.
*The Poor Man and His Parish Church*. Ibid.
*Featherstone's Doom*. Ibid.
*The Figure-Head of the "Caledonia" at her Captain's Grave*. Ibid.
*Sir Beville – The Gate-Song of Stowe*. Ibid
*Modryb Marya – Aunt Mary*. Ibid.
*The Cornish Emigrant's Song*. Ibid.
*The Tamar Spring*. Ibid.
*The Storm*. Ibid.
*A Croon on Hennacliff*. Ibid.
*The Fatal Ship*. Ibid.
*The Doom-Well of St Madron*. Ibid.

## Robert Hunt 1807–1887

Hunt is perhaps now most famous for his 1865 volumes *The Drolls, Traditions, and Superstitions of Old Cornwall: Popular Romances of the West of England (First and Second Series)*, a comprehensive collection of Cornish folktales and folklore. He was born in Plymouth and at one time was Keeper of the Mining Record Office in Cornwall.

From *The Mount's Bay*. Robert Hunt (1829) *The Mount's Bay: A Descriptive Poem*, Penzance: J. Downing and T. Matthews.

## Henry Sewell Stokes 1808–1895

Stokes was born in Truro and worked for much of his life as a solicitor there. He was, however, widely travelled and much published in his day. He eventually became Clerk of the Peace and Clerk of Cornwall County Council.

*The Lady of Place*. Henry Sewell Stokes (1884) *Rhymes from Cornwall*, London: Longmans.
*Life*. W. Herbert Thomas (ed.) (1892) *Poems of Cornwall*, Penzance: F. Rodda.

## Charles Chorley 1810–1874

Chorley was born in Taunton. Sub-editor for the *Royal Cornwall Gazette* for thirty years, he was later editor of the *Journal of the Royal Institution of Cornwall*.

*What Constitutes a Mine?* W.H.K. Wright (ed.) (1896) *West-Country Poets: Their Lives and Works*, London: Elliot Stock.

## William Bentinck Forfar 1810–1895

Forfar was born at Breage and worked as a solicitor in Helston and Plymouth. In his day he was a very popular writer, expanding and developing the tradition of Cornu-English verse.

*The Bal, or, 'Tes a Bra' Keenly Lode*. W. B. Forfar (c.1891) *The Exhibition and other Cornish Poems*. Truro: Netherton and Worth.
*A Dialogue Between Gracey Penrose and Mally Treviskey*. Ibid.

# John Harris 1820–1884

Harris' main achievement was to document the process of industrialisation in Cornwall, yet he was more than just a 'mining' Methodist poet, exploring a wide range of subjects in his verse. Born at Bolenowe, near Camborne, he began work at Dolcoath Mine at the age of twelve.

From *Christian Heroism*. John Harris (1853) *Lays from the Mine, the Moor and the Mountain*. 2nd edition. London: Alexander Heylin.
From *The Mine*. John Harris (1874) *Wayside Pictures, Hymns and Poems*, London: Hamilton, Adams and Co.
*On the Death of my Daughter Lucretia*. Op.cit. (1853)
From *Monro*. John Harris (1879) *Monro*. London: Hamilton, Adams and Co.
From *A Story of Carn Brea*. John Harris (1863) *A Story of Carn Brea, Essays and Poems*. London: Hamilton, Adams and Co.
From *Destruction of the Cornish Tolmen*. Harris, Op.cit. (1874)
*Fall of the Old Mine Stack*. Ibid.
From *The Land's End*. John Harris (1858) *The Land's End, Kynance Cove and Other Poems*. London: Alexander Heylin.
From *Kynance Cove*. Ibid.
*My Infant Daughter Falling Asleep on My Knee*. Ibid.
*On Treslothan Chapel*. Harris Op.cit. (1863)
From *Camborne*. Harris, Op.cit. (1853)
*The Emigrant's Departure*. Ibid.
From *Luda: A Lay of the Druids*. John Harris (1868) *Luda: A Lay of the Druids*. London: Hamilton, Adams and Co.
*Wearing Out*. John Harris (1884) *Last Lays*, Penryn: John Gill.

## Margaret Ann Courtney 1834–1920

Margaret Ann Courtney was born in Penzance and was active as a folklorist and poet. Her most famous work is her 1870 volume *Cornish Feasts and Folklore*. She was also an expert on Cornu-English and in 1880 wrote *A Glossary of Words in Use in West Cornwall*. Most of her poetry incorporates her folkloric knowledge.

*A Picture*. W.H.K. Wright (ed.) (1896) *West-country Poets: Their Lives and Works*. London: Elliot Stock.
*The White Ladie*. W. Herbert Thomas (ed.) (1892) *Poems of Cornwall*, Penzance: F. Rodda.

## Jas Roberts 1838–c.1910

Jas Roberts is the name given on the cover of the publication from which this poem was taken. His name was probably James. He was born at Brillwater, Constantine in 1839 and served as a pupil teacher in the Constantine British School between 1853 and 1857. He then taught in Bradford until 1882.

*A Dirge on Maen Rock*. Jas Roberts (1869) *Dirge on the Tolmen*, Constantine, Cornwall, Roberts: Privately published. Copy held at Morrab Library, Penzance.

## Joseph Thomas 1840–1894

A prolific Anglo-Cornish poet, Thomas was born in Breage and is most famous for his collection *Randigal Rhymes*. He began his career as land surveyor, and then worked as an assistant agent to Sir Edward St Aubyn at Clabor Garden near Mullion.

*Kitty Cornish*. Joseph Thomas (1895) *Randigal Rhymes*, Penzance: F. Rodda.

## Mark Guy Pearse 1842–1930

Born in Camborne, Pearse was a Methodist minister. As well as his many poems and short stories he wrote works for children. Most of his writing was underpinned by Methodism.

*Cornwall*. Mark Guy Pearse (1902) *West Country Songs*, London: Horace Marshall and Son.
*The Miner in Foreign Parts: California.* Ibid.
*The Miner in Foreign Parts: Australia.* Ibid.
*The Fisherman's Song.* Ibid.
*The Hopeless Dawn.* Ibid.

## Katharine Lee Jenner 1854–1936

Katharine Lee Jenner was the wife of Henry Jenner (1848–1934), one of the primary movers of the twentieth-century Cornish Revival. Her work has been somewhat eclipsed by obvious interest in her husband.

*O Mystic Land*. Katharine Lee Jenner (1926) *Songs of the Stars and the Sea*, London: Erskine MacDonald.
*The Old Names.* Ibid.
*Can Gwlasol, Agan Mam-Vro/Anglice, a Patriotic Song For Our Motherland.* Ibid.
*On the Cliff.* Ibid.
*O Lone Grey Land.* Ibid.
*On the Coast (Cornish Fisher-Girl's Lament).* Ibid.
*A Grey Day.* Ibid.
*The Boats of Sennen (Cornish fisher-Girl's Song).* Ibid.
*The Exile.* Ibid.

## Ernest L.T. Harris-Bickford 1859–c.1924.

Bickford was born in Camborne. He was President of the International Literary Association and editor of *Bickford's Magazine*.

*Cornwall's Cliffs.* W.H.K. Wright (ed.) (1896) *West-Country Poets: Their Lives and Works*. London: Elliot Stock.
*Lander's Grave.* W. Herbert Thomas (ed.) (1892) *Poems of Cornwall*, Penzance: F. Rodda.

## James Dryden Hosken 1861–1953

Dryden Hosken was born in Helston. As well as his Anglo-Cornish poetrry he was known for his dramas inspired by Greek culture. He was one of those who were barded at the first Cornish Gorseth at Boscawen Un stone circle in 1928.

*Let Me Hear in My Verses.* James Dryden Hosken (c.1928) *Shores of Lyonesse: Poems Dramatic, Narrative and Lyrical*, London: J.M. Dent.
*When Our Seine Nets Are Dropped in the Bay.* Ibid.
*Porthleven.* James Dryden Hosken (1902) *Poems and Songs of Cornwall*, Plymouth: Mitchell, Burt and Co.
*Phran of Goonhilly.* Op. cit. (c.1928)
*The Land of the West.* Ibid.
*Carminowe and Goonhylda.* Op. cit. (1902)
*Ah! Gwen Carlyon o'er This Heart.* Ibid.
*I Soon Leave Those Eyes of Thine.* Op. cit. (c.1928)
*The Cornish Miner's Funeral.* Ibid.
*Chant of a Cornish Exile.* Ibid.
*One and All.* Op.cit. (1902)
*The Order of the World.* W. Herbert Thomas (ed.) (1892) *Poems of Cornwall*, Penzance: F. Rodda.
*The Sea of Life Doth Ebb.* Op.Cit. (1902)
*Song.* Thomas, *Poems of Cornwall*.

## Arthur Quiller Couch 1863–1944

Quiller Couch came from an old Polperro family and was educated at Oxford, where he began writing under the pseudonym 'Q'. In 1900 he edited the first *Oxford Book of English Verse* and in 1912 became Professor of English at the University of Cambridge. He will be forever associated with Fowey, where he lived and set many of his stories. Contemporary scholarship in Cornwall sees 'Q' as a 'reluctant Cornish revivalist' who initiated debate in his *Cornish Magazine* about the direction Cornwall should take in the twentieth century.

*The Planted Heel*. Arthur Quiller Couch (1929) *Poems*, Oxford: Oxford University Press.
*Sonnet: Isles of Scilly.* Ibid.
*The Harbour of Fowey.* Ibid.
*Helford River.* Ibid.

## John Baragwanath King 1864–1939

John Baragwanath King was born in Penzance and worked as a painter, satirist and poet. In 1928 he contributed a story 'The Laughing Cornishman' to the *Tre, Pol and Pen Annual* and was made a bard of the Cornish Gorseth in 1930, taking the name  Baragwanath (Wheaten Bread).

*Celtic Perversity*. Baragwanath King (1925) *Arthur and Others in Cornwall*, London: Erskine MacDonald.
*Mary of Halveggan Down.* Ibid

## W. Herbert Thomas 1866–1951

W. Herbert Thomas came from St Day. At the age of 21 he tried his fortune in California and worked as a reporter in San Francisco. He later became a staffer on the *Cornishman* newspaper. Thomas edited the hugely influential collection *Poems of Cornwall*, which he hoped would remind homesick emigrants of the 'rocky land of strangers'.

*All Hail! Old Cornwall!* W. Herbert Thomas (ed.) (1892) *Poems of Cornwall*, Penzance: F. Rodda.
*Entombed!* W. Herbert Thomas (1893) *Entombed! A poem of the Dolcoath Disaster,* Camborne: Camborne Printing and Stationery.
*In a Cornish Lane.* W. Herbert Thomas (1898) *Among Cornish Fisher Folk*, Camborne: Camborne Printing and Stationery.
*The Gurnard's Head.* Ibid.
*Sunset from Bodmin Beacon.* Ibid.

## Anonymous [published1869]

Anonymous (1869) *Broadsheet giving Lines on the Terrible Accident at the Old Delabole Slate Quarries.*

## Annie E. Argall c.1876–c.1916

The daughter of a photographer, Annie E. Argall was born in Truro and began writing poetry in her teens. Her poetry was widely published in Cornish magazines and newspapers.

*The Charm of Beauty*. W.H.K. Wright (ed.) (1896), *West-country Poets: Their Lives and Works*. London: Elliot Stock.
*The Fal*. W. Herbert Thomas (ed.) (1892) *Poems of Cornwall*, Penzance: F. Rodda.

## Anonymous [Ms 1913]

Anonymous (1913) *The Clay Strike – the White Country Dispute*. Photocopy of typed manuscript in editor's own collection.

## Anonymous [published 1919]

Anonymous (1919) *Levant Mine Disaster, Monday October 20th 1919, A Poem and the Names and Addresses of 31 Miners who lost their lives.* Collection of the editor.

# Notes

## Andrew Boorde
*Iche Cham a Cornyshe Man*
1. This poem forms the appendix to the first chapter on Cornwall and Cornishmen in Furnivall.
2. I am a Cornishman, ale I can brew;
   It will make one to cack, also to spew;
   It is thick and smoky, and also it is thin;
   It is like wash that pigs had wrestled in.
   I cannot brew, nor dress flesh, nor fish;
   Many folk do say I mar many a good dish.
   Shut the door, mate! I have something to say,
       "When old knaves are dead, young knaves will play."
   I am all a-hungered, I swear by my faith
   I have not eaten meat since yesterday;
   I would like to share a story amid the cup;
   Give me a quart of ale that I may sup.
   Aye, good mate, I have at home, fish and also tin;
   Drink mate, with me, or else I shall begin.
   God! What great cold and hunger I do abide!
   Will you, friend, come home at the next tide?
   I pray God to direct him to travel well,
   That when he comes home, me he will not kill
   For putting a straw through his great net.
   Another pint of ale, mate, now fetch me,
   For my mate will go to London to try at the law,
   To sue Tre, Pol and Pen, for wagging of a straw.
   Now, mate, farewell! I can no longer abide;
   I must go over to the ale house at the other side;
   And now come with me, mate, I pray,
   And let us make merry as long as we may.

## Nicholas Roscarrock
*A Sonnet*
1. This sonnet forms a preface to Roscarrock's *Lives*. As in the two other Roscarrock poems which follow, for the sake of clarity, some spellings have been altered.

*A Friendly Warning about Saints*
2. This poem forms the second part of the preface to the *Lives*.

*Of Saint Aaron*
3. Saint Aaron is the first saint catalogued. Unlike the rest of the collection, Roscarrock chooses to tell the life of this saint in verse.

## Richard Carew
*Prosopopeia*
1. This poem introduces the *Survey*. It is a pun – with the book itself supposed to be speaking.

*The Well of St Keyne*
2. It is said that whichever partner of a newly-married couple drinks from the well will dominate the other. The poet Robert Southey (1774–1843) also wrote a poem about it.

*The River Lynher*
3. As his *Survey* tells us, Carew was a keen fisherman.
4. *chevisance* – power.
5. *Oceanus* – the god of the great water in Greek mythology.
6. *Tellus* – the Roman goddess of the earth and fertility.
7. *Argus* – a giant with a hundred eyes.
8. *Phoebus* – one of the names of Apollo.

*Epitaph for John Arundell*
9. The Arundells were a notable Cornish family.

*From A Herring's Tail*
10. This epic poem is an Arthurian satire, with Sir Lymazon (Latin, *limax*: a snail) battling the winds high on a a weathercock above Tintagel castle.

*Full Thirteen Five of Years*
11. These lines were written immediately before Carew's death and were found by

his grandson Alexander Carew. They were
used as his epitaph.

## Michael Drayton
From *First Song, Poly-Olbion*
1   *Brute* – this refers to Brutus, the Trojan,
    who in mythology divided the kingdom of
    Britain among his three sons.
2   *Thetis* – a sea nymph in Greek mythology.
3   *Bresan* – a small island near Land's End.
4   *chersonese* – a place almost surrounded
    by the sea.
5   *Hoar-rock in the wood* – this is a
    translation of the traditional Cornish name
    of St Michael's Mount, Cara Clowse in
    Cowse.
6   *Loo* — Loe Pool near Porthleven.
7   *Menedge* – Meneage. This is the northern
    area of the Lizard peninsula.
8   *Roseland* – The Roseland peninsula, an
    area running from Tregony to St Anthony's
    Head.

## Thomas Hogg
*Godolphin*
1   This poem recalls events of the 1595
    Spanish invasion of Paul, Mousehole,
    Newlyn and Penzance by the Spanish. The
    invasion was repelled by Sir Francis
    Godolphin.
*Witchcraft*
2   Prefixed to the copy of this book in the
    British Museum, is a note, signed H.,
    stating that 'this is a satire on the Cornish
    historian, notwithstanding his assumed
    adherence to veracity'.
3   *Tolpedon* – in Cornish this is spelt *tol pedn*
    and means 'holed headland'.
4   *Silura* – this probably refers to the Celtic
    peoples of south-east Wales who put up a
    strong defence against the Romans.
5   *Whitaker* – A reference to the Manchester-
    based historian John Whitaker, who wrote
    extensively on the religious history of
    Cornwall. See note 2.

## Humphry Davy
*In Ludgvan Churchyard*
1   Several members of Davy's family were
    buried at Ludgvan, near Penzance. The
    poem was written in 1795.
*The Sons of Genius*
2   This poem was written when Davy was
    apprenticed to a surgeon in Penzance.
*Mount's Bay*
3   *Bolerium* – Roman expression for the

Land's End peninsula. It is probably from
the Greek explorer Pytheas, who named
the region Belerion ('shining one').
4   *Theora* – According to legend an Irish
    vessel was shipwrecked on the rock Pedn-
    men-du (Headland of the Black Rock) and
    all aboard perished, except Theora, who
    managed to scramble onto the rock. She,
    too, could not be rescued and perished.

## George Woodley
*Ode to Cornubia*
1   This is a slightly edited version of the
    introductory ode to Cornubia.
2   *Hensb'rough* – Hensbarrow Down, upland
    area above St Austell, where much of the
    present-day china clay mining industry is
    found.
*Roche Rock and Hermitage*
3   Roche Rock is just outside the village of
    Roche.
*Botallack*
4   Botallack Mine is near the village of
    Pendeen in West Cornwall. It is famous for
    its two engine houses perched
    precariously on the cliffside and the
    network of shafts which once went under
    the ocean bed.

## Henry Quick
*The Life and Progress of Henry Quick of
Zennor*
1   An acrostic spelling out Henry Quick.
*The Death of Pascoe Semmens, 1826*
2   An acrostic spelling out Pascoe Semmens.
*The Death of John Martyns, 1836*
3   Poems such as this were to have an
    enormous influence on other later disaster
    verses.

## John Tabois Tregellas
From St *Agnes Bear Hunt*
1   *biddixes*– pickaxes .
2   *gad* – a pointed wedge used at the rock-
    face.
3   *dag* – a kind of hatchet used by miners.
4   *Cousin Jackies* – the name applied to
    Cornishmen living away from Cornwall.
5   *hingun* – engine.
6   *kibble* – a kind of bucket used for lowering
    up and down the shaft.
7   *whem* – whim – a machine used for raising
    ore.
8   *tutwork men* – labourers being paid a
    particular price for a job.
9   *tributer* – a miner whose pay is a

proportion of the ores mined.

10 *halvaner* – a worker whose task is to remove impurities from ores, halvans being ore not ready for sale.

11 *buddles* – conical devices in which tin is washed to remove impurities.

12 *trunks* – long pits in which impurities are separated.

13 *covers* – boxes into which the ore falls from the rock-face: they are found at the head of the trunks.

14 *cobbin' hammers* – hammers used to break ore.

15 *coors* – a workshift.

16 *stem-man* – a dayshift labourer.

## William Sandys

*Visit to Lunnon*

1 *Sos* – opinion varies on the meaning of this phrase, used by many Cornish people of the period as a term of endearment. It may be derived from soster (sister). It appears to have been used self-deprecatingly.

2 *Lunnon* – London.

3 *quilkins* – frog.

4 *padgitepooe* – newt.

5 *tummals* – plenty of.

6 *bedoled* – pained.

7 *fitty* – proper.

8 *buch-a-boo* – a ghost or a goblin.

9 *man ingine* – device for lowering or raising men in a mine.

10 *St. Joost* – St Just-in-Penwith.

11 *Loggan* – probably a reference to the Logan Stone near Treen in West Cornwall: loggan means to rock.

12 *poldavy* – sail canvas.

13 *mabyers* – May birds.

## Charles Taylor Stephens

From *The Chief of Barat-Anac*

1 Zennor Quoit and its imaginary history form the subject-matter of this epic poem. It seems to have been written a good deal earlier than 1862.

## Robert Stephen Hawker

*The Song of Western Men*

1 This poem is most commonly known now as Trelawny and is Cornwall's national anthem. It is based on the colourful life of Sir Jonathan Trelawny, referring to the imprisonment of him and six other bishops by James II.

The rebellion alluded to in the poem never happened.

*The Sea*

2 This poem is actually incomplete. It was written while Hawker was still a teenager.

*The Silent Tower of Bottreau*

3 Bottreau, or Boscastle Churcn does not have any bells. Bells were once shipped to the church but the blasphemy of the captain of the ship unleashed the events of the poem.

4 *chough* – a bird which is said to hold the spirit of King Arthur. It is unwise and unlucky to kill one.

*The Western Shore*

5 *Morwenna* – the founding saint of Hawker's church at Morwenstow.

*The Poor Man and his Parish Church*

6 Hawker confronts what he considered to be the excesses and consequences of Methodist reform in Cornwall.

*Featherstone's Doom*

7 The Blackrock lies in the middle of Widemouth Bay, near Bude. It is said to be haunted by Featherstone the wrecker who is imprisoned there.

*The Figure-Head of the "Caledonia" at her Captain's Grave*

8 The figurehead can still be seen in Morwenstow churchyard.

*Sir Beville – The Gate-Song of Stowe*

9 Sir Beville Grenville (1594–1643) was a Cornish Royalist commander during the Civil War. He lived at Stowe, near Morwenstow, and was killed at Lansdown.

*Modryb Marya – Aunt Mary*

10 The title of this poem is in Cornish: it translates as Aunt Mary. For commentary, see Alan M. Kent and Tim Saunders (eds.) (2000) *Looking at the Mermaid: A Reader in Cornish Literature 900–1900*, London: Francis Boutle.

*The Tamar Spring*

11 The Tamar's source is in the parish of Morwenstow.

*A Croon on Hennacliff*

12 Highly critical of the failure of the Bude life-boatmen to save the stricken vessel Bencoolen in 1862.

*The Fatal Ship*

13 Based on the sinking of H.M.S. Captain, an ironclad vessel lost off Cape Finisterre in 1870.

14 *Yahvah* – an alternative spelling of Jehovah.

*The Doom-Well of St Madron*

15  The Holy Well at Madron in West Cornwall is reputed to have magic powers.
16  *but and ben* – an old phrase for butlery and hall.
17  *Routorr* – Rough Tor.

## Robert Hunt
From *The Mount's Bay*

1  *Landewednack* – this probably means the church-site of St Winwalo; it refers to a place on the Lizard peninsula.
2  *Cimmerian* – people of the ancient world said to live north of the Black Sea. In post-Renaissance times the word was associated with Celtic peoples like the Cornish.

## Henry Sewell Stokes
*The Lady of Place*

1  This poem celebrates the life of Elizabeth Treffry, a courageous Cornish heroine who rallied the men of Fowey in 1457, in the absence of her husband, to stand against the invasion of her community and her home, the fortified castle occupied to this day by the Treffry family.
2  *Cornish hug* – reference to Cornish wrestling that later came to indicate Cornish prowess in battle and combat.
3  *Grace Darling* was famous for rescuing five people from the wreck of the Forfarshire steamboat.

## William Bentinck Forfar
From *The Bal, or, 'Tes a Bra' Keenly Lode*

1  *bal* – a mine.
2  *phospheric light* – a light of this kind is sometimes seen at night, showing where a lode is close to the surface.
3  *gozan* – an iron and quartz peroxide.
4  *mundic* – another name for iron pyrites.
5  *kiddle-e-wink* – an unlicensed beer shop.
*A Dialogue between Gracey Penrose and Mally Treviskey*
6  *vaist* – Cornu-English for feast. Feast days are popular occasions in Cornwall.
7  *stompses* – stamps, devices for crushing ore.
8  *maazedgerry* would appear to be mean someone who is angry and useless; *mazed* meaning mad or angry.
9  *midjans* – pieces.
10  *jouds* – rags.
11  *buzz* – an earthenware pot.
12  *steave* – to freeze.

## John Harris
From *Christian Heroism*

1  This poem was based on a real incident of bravery underground. It is the end sequence of a longer poem which begins with John Wesley's coming to Cornwall.
From *The Mine*
2  *adit* – a horizontal tunnel which allows water to either be pumped or to drain out of a mine.
3  *winze* – a passage allowing communication and ventilation between one lode and another.
4  *killas* – clay slate.
5  *start* – where the mineral begins to be found.
6  *giggers* – those engaged in surface work.
7  *lander* – the workman who receives the bucket at the top of the shaft.
8  *mineral-sprite* – probably a reference to Knockers or Knockies, little people who live underground in Cornish folklore.
9  *spars* – white minerals, usually crystalline, such as quartz or felspar.
10  *stope* – the location where horizontal extraction occurs.
11  *rize* – where the extraction process has dug upwards.
12  *tributer* – a miner whose pay is a proportion of the ores mined.
13  *stull* – where timber is put in the backs of levels to support falling rubbish.
*On the Death of my Daughter Lucretia*
14  Harris' second daughter Lucretia died at Christmas 1855. Her death haunted him throughout the remainder of his life.
15  *reenes* – a spur of land.
From *Monro*
16  Harris' epic autobiographical poem.
From *A Story of Carn Brea*
17  *Carn Brea* is the upland area south of the Camborne-Pool-Redruth conurbation.
From *Kynance Cove*
18  *Kynance Cove* is at the south-west tip of the Lizard peninsula and was a popular destination for travellers in the nineteenth century.
*On Treslothan Chapel*
19  *Treslothan Chapel*, near Troon, is where Harris and his family are buried. This section is from the longer poem on Carn Brea.
From *Luda: A Lay of the Druids*
20  *gorseddau-seat* – a Gorseth seat or throne. In his notes on the poem Harris calls it 'a seat of judgment'.
21  *a hook of gold* – a sickle.

## Jas Roberts
*A Dirge on Maen Rock*
1   The rock was demolished on 9 March 1869.
2   *Tregeagle* refers to Jan Tregeagle, the Cornish 'Faust'. Famously he was given the tasks of emptying Dozmary Pool with a holed limpet shell, then to weave a rope made of sand.

## Joseph Thomas
*Kitty Cornish*
1   *gook* – the name of the headgear worn by women at work in Cornwall.
2   *nuddick* – the neck.
3   *haggalans* – haw berries.
4   *towser* – a hessian apron.
5   *mooling* – kneading.
6   *fuggan* – cake.

## Mark Guy Pearse
*The Miner in Foreign Parts: California*
1   *bal that's knacked* – an abandoned mine.
*The Miner in Foreign Parts: Australia*
2   The name Zacky was popularly applied to the typical Cornish miner.
*The Hopeless Dawn*
3   Pearse was probably inspired by Frank Bramley's painting of loss at sea, 'A Hopeless Dawn' (1888).

## Katharine Lee Jenner
*The Old Names*
1   The calling of the *Gwynver* refers to the sound of the sea breaking upon Gwynver Sands at Sennen. The sea is said to moan for the loss of Guinevere, who escaped from the sands when Lyonesse was submerged. The sound portends ill-fortune.
*Can Gwlasol, Agan Mam-Vro/Anglice, A Patriotic Song for our Motherland*
2   *One and All* – the motto of Cornwall.

## Ernest L.T. Harris-Bickford
*Lander's Grave*
1   The grave of the Cornish explorer Richard Lander was at Fernando Po, off the coast of West Africa.

## James Dryden Hosken
*Porthleven*
1   *Halzephron* is on the Lizard

peninsula. The name clearly derives from the Cornish – *aulz effarn* – Hell Cliff.
*Phran of Goonhilly*
2   *Phran* has nothing to do with the Cornish saint, Piran.
*Carminowe and Goonhylda*
3   *Carminowe* comes from *carn menow*, probably meaning a 'stoney outcrop'. Goonhylda is Hosken's interpretation of Goonhilly (*goon helhy*) meaning 'downs of hunting'.
*Ah! Gwen Carlyon o'er This Heart*
4   It is unclear who Gwen Carlyon is.
*The Cornish Miner's Funeral*
5   *Wendron* is between Camborne and Helston.
*Chant of a Cornish Exile*
6   Here a miner remembers home.
*One and All*
7   *Grammar* and *Jan,* like *Zacky*, are stock names for Cornish characters.
8   A reference to the wrestling match between the Corineus (mythical founder of Cornwall) and the giant Gogmagog on Plymouth Hoe. Corineus beat the giant by forcing him onto the rocks below.
9   *Cousin Jack* – the name applied to any Cornishman working outside Cornwall that has also come to signify Cornishmen overseas.

## Arthur Quiller Couch
*The Planted Heel*
1   Talland Church lies close to Polperro.

## John Baragwanath King
*Celtic Perversity*
1   *St Joseph* – Joseph of Arimathea.
2   *King Alfred* is the king referred to here.
3   The Provost Marshall was Sir Anthony Kingston and the mayor was Nicholas Boyer.

## W. Herbert Thomas
*All Hail! Old Cornwall!*
1   Cornwall may be translated as 'the horn of strangers'.
2   Cornish tin in an alloy of bronze was reputedly use to decorate the Temple of Solomon.
*Entombed!*
3   This poem appeared in *The Cornishman* newspaper a few days

after the accident occurred on 20 September 1893.

## Anonymous [published 1869]
*Lines on the Terrible Accident at the Old Delabole Slate Quarries, 1869*
1   *papote head* – device at the top of the quarry to assist in lifting slate.

## Anonymous [Ms 1913]
*The Clay Strike – the White Country Dispute*
1   The clay strike is one of the most fascinating events in the history of Trade Unionism in Cornwall. Various writers have been put forward as the author of this poem, but the evidence is inconclusive. On the clay strike, see Alan M. Kent, 'The Cornish Alps: resisting romance in the clay country' in Ella Westland (ed.) (1997) *Cornwall: The Cultural Construction of Place,* Penzance: The Patten Press.

## Anonymous [published 1919]
*The Levant Mine Disaster*
1   Perhaps the most famous Cornish mining accident. The upper portion of the man-engine, carrying 30 men, fell 46 fathoms.

# Further reading

Brendon, Piers (1975) *Hawker of Morwenstow*, London: Cape.

Dunstan, Ralph (ed.) (c.1932) *Cornish Dialect and Folk Songs*, Truro: Jordan's Bookshop.

Halliday, F.E. (1967) *A Cornish Chronicle: The Carews of Antony from Armada to Civil War*, Newton Abbot: David & Charles.

Hardie, Melissa (ed.) (1992) *A Mere Interlude: Some Literary Visitors in Lyonesse*, Penzance: The Patten Press.

Hawkey, Muriel (ed.) (1948) *A Cornish Chorus: A Collection of Prose and Verse*, London: Westaway Books.

Headdon, Bill (ed.) (1995) *Cornish Links/Kevrennow Kernewek*, Tunbridge Wells: Kernow Poets Press.

Hechter, Michael (1975) *Internal Colonialism: The Celtic Fringe in British National Development, 1536–1966*, London: Routledge and Kegan Paul.

Jenkin, A.K. Hamilton (1972 [1927]) *The Cornish Miner*, Newton Abbot: David & Charles.

McGrady, Richard (1993) *Traces of Ancient Mystery: The Ballad Carols of Davies Gilbert and William Sandys*, Redruth: Institute of Cornish Studies.

Murdoch, Brian (1993) *Cornish Literature*, Cambridge: D.S. Brewer.

Newman, Paul (1994) *The Meads of Love: The Life and Poetry of John Harris*, Redruth: Dyllansow Truran.

Pearson, A. (1976) *Robert Hunt F.R.S.*, Penzance: The Federation of Old Cornwall Societies.

Phillipps, K.C. (1976) *Westcountry Words and Ways*, Newton Abbot: David & Charles.

Pool, P.A.S. (1984) *The Life and Progress of Henry Quick of Zennor*, Redruth: Dyllansow Truran.

Rowe, John (1993 [1953]) *Cornwall in the Age of the Industrial Revolution*. St Austell: Cornish Hillside Publications.

Saunders, Tim (1999) *The Wheel: An Anthology of Modern Poetry in Cornish 1850–1980*, London: Francis Boutle.

Shaw, Thomas (1967) *A History of Cornish Methodism*, Truro: Bradford Barton.

Thomas, D.M. (ed.) (1970) *The Granite Kingdom: Poems of Cornwall*, Bradford Barton.

Trewin, J.C. (ed.) (1948) *Robert Stephen Hawker: Footprints of Former Men in Far Cornwall 1870*, London: Westaway Books.

Val Baker, Denys (1980) *The Spirit of Cornwall*, London: W.H. Allen.

Wakelin, Martyn (1975) *Language and History in Cornwall*, Leicester: Leicester University Press.